HEROES AND MARTYRS

OF

GEORGIA.

GEORGIA'S RECORD

IN THE

REVOLUTION OF 1861.

By JAMES M. FOLSOM.

MACON, GA.:
BURKE, BOYKIN & COMPANY.
1864.

Original Title Page of Heroes and Martyrs of Georgia.

From the Special Collections Division, University of Georgia Libraries.

HEROES AND

MARTYRS

OF

GEORGIA

Heroes and Martyrs

OF

GEORGIA

———— ⟨⟨⟩⟩ ————

GEORGIA'S RECORD

IN THE

REVOLUTION OF 1861.

By James Madison Folsom.

Macon, GA.:
Burke, Boykin & Company.
1864.

New Materials Copyright 1995

ISBN 0-935523-49-9

Reprinted in 1995
as the fourth volume of
the *Army of Northern Virginia Series*

by

BUTTERNUT AND BLUE
3411 Northwind Road
Baltimore, Maryland 21234
410-256-9220

The Errata contained on page 161 in this book is corrected from the original.

INTRODUCTION

In a March 21, 1865 review of *Heroes and Martyrs of Georgia: Georgia's Record in the Revolution of 1861*, the editor of the Milledgeville *Confederate Union* implored the future historian to "build upon the foundation which the modest author of the little volume before us has furnished."[1] Unfortunately, the extreme scarcity of the book has left it unknown to all but a very small number of those chronicling the exploits of the Army of Northern Virginia. This neglect is unfortunate, since *Heroes and Martyrs* stands as an invaluable contemporary source on the campaigns and battles of Robert E. Lee's fabled army.

The author of *Heroes and Martyrs*, James Madison Folsom, Jr., was born on February 10, 1838, in Savannah, Georgia, the second child of James Madison Folsom (1807-1852) and Mary Caroline Haupter Folsom (1812-1861). A native of Exeter, New Hampshire, the elder Folsom had ventured south in his early years, living first in Charleston, South Carolina, where he met and married his wife in 1834, and then in Savannah. "A bookbinder, bookseller, and merchant," as well as a militia officer and Democratic politician, James Sr. left Savannah sometime in the late 1830s or 1840s and moved his family to the small community of Gordon in Wilkinson County, Georgia.[2]

Gordon, located on the Central Georgia Railroad in the central portion of Georgia's black belt, boasted in 1849 "two stores, one tavern, one blacksmith, and one physician." The town also received a considerable share of the cotton crop raised in Wilkinson and the adjacent counties.[3] Among those undoubtedly sending cotton into the town was James Folsom, Sr., who is listed as a farmer in the 1850 census with eight hundred dollars worth of real estate. (Although the census does not list the value of Folsom's personal estate, the 1850 Wilkinson County slave schedules indicate that he owned two individuals, a twenty-nine-year-old man and an eleven-year-old boy.) Living with James Sr. were his wife, oldest son Robert Warren (1835-1864), also a farmer, James Jr., and daughter Maria Dudley (1840-1875). All three children attended school during the census year.[4]

By 1860, the two Folsom sons had left their sister and widowed mother and moved from Wilkinson into adjacent Twiggs

i

County. While Robert practiced medicine (owning five hundred dollars in personal estate in 1860), his brother James taught school and boarded in the household of Simeon Tharpe. Tharpe's farm was near Marion, a community six miles west of the Twiggs County seat of Jeffersonville.[5]

James Folsom, Jr., an "original secessionist" according to a Folsom family history, apparently had some standing in Twiggs County, for by the end of 1860 he commanded a local military company known as the "Twiggs Volunteers." Residents in Burke County, Georgia, located just south of Augusta, also probably knew of Folsom, for there on February 27, 1861, he married Mary M. Roberts in the residence of her guardian, planter Ephraim Ponder. Mary, seventeen years old at the time of her wedding, owned fifteen thousand dollars in personal estate in 1860, much of it in the form of seven adult and four adolescent and infant slaves.[6]

The newlyweds returned after their nuptials to Twiggs County where, as captain of the Volunteers, James Folsom encountered problems plaguing many other military officers across the South. In December 1860, only weeks before his state's secession, Folsom wrote Georgia Governor Joseph E. Brown urgently requesting one hundred Mississippi Rifles for his company. If these guns were not available, Folsom stood ready to accept smoothbore muskets.[7]

By the spring of 1861 Folsom faced apparent dissension in the ranks of his company. On April 1, he wrote Governor Brown complaining that the Twiggs Volunteers had been disgraced by the company's first lieutenant, Simeon Tharpe. (Whether Folsom still lived in Tharpe's household at this time is unknown.) Tharpe had written the governor informing him not to order out the Volunteers "as most of the company are men of famileys and poor men, and that it was their wish to remain at home."

Folsom vehemently denied the assertions of his lieutenant, stating that with the exception of Tharpe and his overseer, Benjamin F. Southall, every man in the Volunteers had expressed "a perfect willingness to go to fight the battles of their country at any time or place." Having already written Brown about his personal willingness to fight, Folsom closed his letter by asking that his company be given a place in a contingent of troops being sent to Pensacola, Florida, to bolster the forces besieging Fort Pickens.[8]

Within a little more than three weeks after writing the governor about his men's eagerness to fight, Folsom's company, including Tharpe and Southall, had left Twiggs County. The men were bound not for Florida, but Virginia. Arriving in Augusta, Georgia, on April 25, the Volunteers received arms and mustered into Confederate service, being designated Company C, Fourth Georgia Volunteer Infantry Regiment.[9] It was perhaps also at this time that Folsom's men became known as the "Jorees." According to Private John W. West, a member of the Twiggs Volunteers, the nom de guerre came from the company's uniforms, which "having three black stripes upon the tail of the coat" resembled the three black feathers on the bird called "Joree."[10]

The "Jorees" left Augusta along with the balance of the Fourth Georgia on May 2, bound for the Navy Yard at Portsmouth, Virginia. On May 9, the regiment completed its organization by holding formal elections for officers. Folsom retained his position as head of Company C. By the end of May, the Fourth Georgia had moved from Portsmouth to a site in Suffolk County located between Pig Point and Craney Island which became known as Camp Jackson. There the regiment remained for nearly a year, performing infantry and artillery drills and building bridges, fortifications, signal stations, and eventually winter quarters.

Captain Folsom greatly helped make the Fourth Georgia "a splendid body of soldiers," according to the regiment's official history.[11] By June 30, 1861, however, Folsom was down with chronic inflammatory rheumatism and spent at least two months lying on his back. The stricken captain returned to Georgia sometime in the fall of 1861 and by the first of October had sent to the Confederate Secretary of War a letter resigning his officer's commission. In the same enclosure Folsom included a letter from Colonel George P. Doles of the Fourth Georgia, tendering through the Confederate Secretary of War the captain's resignation to the Governor of Georgia. Folsom had apparently failed to request resignation from the Confederate War Department prior to his decision, a bureaucratic oversight that irritated Confederate Secretary of War Judah Benjamin.

In an October 3 letter to Georgia's Governor Brown, Benjamin fumed that officers like Folsom seemed to be "totally unaware that their muster into the service of the Confederate States forms a contract as binding on them as on this Government." Such men "had no more right to leave the service before the expiration of their term, without the consent of the Government, than the Government has to turn them out of office without cause." Benjamin requested that Brown inform Folsom of his "grave error" which "amounts technically to desertion," although the secretary felt sure such was not the intention of Captain Folsom. The matter had been cleared up by November 6, 1861, when the Secretary of War officially notified Georgia's adjutant general that Folsom's resignation had been accepted.[12]

At the same time Folsom breached bureaucratic protocol he also sent through Colonel Doles another letter to the Confederate Secretary of War. In the latter missive, dated October 8 and written from Gordon, Georgia, Folsom asked permission "to raise a Battalion of Guerillas for the war." According to the letter, Folsom had previous experience in guerilla warfare and felt satisfied that he "could wage it with success." Hoping to raise, mount, arm, and equip a battalion of at least five companies, the late infantry captain desired to "cooperate with Genls Lee Floyd & Wise in North Western Virginia."

Five days after Folsom sent this request, Secretary of War Benjamin replied that he would accept "a company or a Battalion of mounted men electing their own officers and fully armed and equipped." The war department would not allow Folsom to decide where the company would serve. Benjamin would also refuse to accept the company if by "guerillas" Folsom meant that his command would "be in any respect independent of the laws of military organization and command."[13]

Although Folsom never raised his guerilla command, he apparently still sought ways to aid the Confederate cause. Shortly after the passage of the Conscription Act in the spring of 1862, Folsom wrote the Confederate Secretary of State, tendering his services to assist in enrolling conscripts in extreme southeast Georgia. Writing from Doctortown, a community located along the Altamaha River, Folsom also mentioned that he had "the honor of holding a commission as aide de camp (with the rank of Col.) to Governor Brown." "Independant of pay," Folsom wished no remuneration for his services.[14]

As a twenty-four-year-old white male, Folsom was himself liable to conscription and received a number of visits from the Appling County, Georgia, enrolling officer in the spring and summer of 1862. When the enrolling officer made his first round, he exempted the ex-captain from conscription due to "lameness." On the officer's second round, he left a notification at Folsom's house that the young man had been enrolled as a conscript.

Folsom reacted to his draft notice with a panicked letter to Governor Brown dated August 26, 1862. Folsom seemed incredulous that he, a "confirmed cripple," would be conscripted. He furthermore mentioned his November 7, 1860, appointment as aide-de-camp to the Governor. If this commission were still in effect, Folsom argued, it made him "a Civil as well as Military officer...who may at any time be called into active service and is by your order exempt from the Confederate service."

Folsom ended his letter by arguing that he was not "trying to quibble" himself out of the operation of the Conscript Act. Still afflicted with rheumatism, he claimed that "by the slightest weather" he was "stricken down." "I am now talking for my life your excellency," he pleaded, "one night in a camp at Marietta will take it."

Brown's responded by stating that Folsom had vacated his position on the governor's staff by voluntarily accepting a commission in the Confederate army. The governor regretted Folsom's affliction, but could do nothing since "the question of disability is determined by the Surgeons." Despite the governor's lack of assistance, Folsom ultimately eluded the conscription officer, as there is no record of him serving again in the Confederate Army.[15]

Exempt from military duty, Folsom apparently turned to writing and publishing, activities he undoubtedly had learned about from his father. By early May 1864, Folsom had applied for a copyright in the clerk's office of the District Court of the Confederate States for the Southern district of Georgia for a series of book that would bear the title *Heroes and Martyrs of Georgia*. The work's publisher was Burke, Boykin, and Company of Macon, Georgia, one of the Empire State's leading publishing firms and an extensive publisher of local authors.[16]

Folsom initially intended *Heroes and Martyrs* to be a four-volume work offering "the Statistical and Historical Record of each Regiment from Georgia." He collected some of the material for this work in a trip to Virginia probably made during the spring of 1864. (James's sister Maria may have accompanied him, as she was present in the camp of the Fourteenth Georgia Infantry in late March visiting her other brother, Colonel Robert Folsom.[17]) The bulk of Folsom's manuscript, the unit histories compiled by regimental officers, came to him in the mail, most having been written in the summer of 1864 while in the trenches at Petersburg, Virginia.[18]

Numerous problems plagued Folsom's attempts to gather accurate and complete information about Georgia Confederate units. When he contacted the colonel of the Sixty-Fourth Georgia Infantry, John W. Evans, to obtain statistical data about the regiment, Evans replied on July 29, 1864, that he would forward the material. On July 30, Evans died leading his men in an attack at the Crater. Folsom believed that after the colonel's death, the statistics that he had compiled "were lost or mislaid."

Incessant marching and changing of position often led to the loss of regimental records, as was the case with the Nineteenth Georgia Infantry. In some instances, especially with cavalry regiments, excessive mobility and inefficient mail service left Folsom unable to contact units. Thus was the case with the Phillips' Legion Cavalry, whose cursory unit history in *Heroes and Martyrs* only runs through the end of 1863.[19]

The greatest obstacle to the completion of Folsom's work was the Union army, specifically the two corps of William T. Sherman's Army commanded by General O. O. Howard which passed through Folsom's hometown of Gordon on November 22-24, 1864. (Folsom undoubtedly lived at the time in the house of his late mother who had died in the summer of 1861.) Northern soldiers either carried off or destroyed the bulk of Folsom's manuscript materials, including all of the unit histories he had collected from the Army of Tennessee.[20]

Despite these losses, volume one of *Heroes and Martyrs* first appeared for sale in early February 1865. Not surprisingly, Folsom had problems distributing the book. In an advertisement running in several major Georgia newspapers in February and March 1865, the author noted that poor communications had not enabled him to send copies of the volume to its many subscribers in the Army of Northern Virginia. Some of these soldiers had requested that the volumes be delivered to their families. Attempting to oblige these requests, Folsom urged anyone having relations or friends of men in Lee's Army to send for their copies "as soon as possible, before this edition is exhausted by public sale." The subscription price for those who had not reserved a copy was ten dollars.[21]

The paperbound volume Folsom sent to subscribers contained a wealth of information on thirteen of Georgia's infantry regiments, two infantry battalions, one cavalry battalion, and one artillery battalion. Although he had hoped to include more "incidents of personal heroism," Folsom still managed to list the names of a number of men distinguished for gallantry. One of the few individuals dealt with at considerable length was the eldest Folsom brother, Robert. Nicknamed "Cedar Run" by his men in recognition of his heroic conduct at that engagement, Colonel Robert Folsom elicited substantial praise throughout his military career from those serving both above and below him. (The aspiring young officer felt the praise was well-deserved; in the fall of 1862 he wrote his sister that "stranger things have happened in this world than my elevation to the wreath of brigadier.") Colonel Folsom's death on the morning of May 6, 1864, in the battle of the Wilderness deprived Lee's Army of one of its best regimental commanders.[22]

Hoping to publicize *Heroes and Martyrs*, James Folsom promised to send copies of his volume to any newspaper editor who published his advertisement. The book received notice from several editors, including those of the Milledgeville *Confederate Union* and *Southern Recorder*. The editor of the *Recorder*, noting that the volume had been "gotten up with [as] much care and accuracy as the nature of the cases would admit" urged its compiler "to sit himself down" to the task of rewriting those sketches destroyed by the Yankees. Both editors commended the work to the public and wished the author the best in his future efforts. The editor of the *Macon Daily Telegraph* stated that the book was "invaluable" as a record, proclaiming that "every family in Georgia should possess a copy."[23]

Appearing only a few months before the units it chronicled disbanded, *Heroes and Martyrs of Georgia* was a financial disaster. In an article published in 1932 entitled "Book became a Frankenstein," Wilkinson County, Georgia historian Victor Davidson states that James Folsom had borrowed seven thousand dollars in November 1864 to finance the publication of his book, in the process mortgaging land and a house he owned in Gordon. Wilkinson County Superior Court Deed Records verify Davidson's assertion. Folsom struggled for several years after the war to pay this and other debts, but was unable to do so. In June 1868, he authorized the sale of all the buildings and property he owned to pay off more than three thousand dollars in debts.[24]

With no property left in Georgia, Folsom and his wife moved in 1869 to the town of Camden in south-central Arkansas. Living there in 1870 was Folsom's sister, Maria, who had married a Confederate veteran, Charles Augustine Bridewell (1838-1917). (Bridewell had served from August to November 1864 as a captain and assistant quartermaster in the Confederate hospitals in Milledgeville, only nineteen miles north of Maria's hometown of Gordon. It was undoubtedly during this time that the couple had first gotten acquainted.)

Charles Bridewell was a lawyer and James Folsom apparently entered into a partnership with his brother-in-law. The 1870 Ouachita County, Arkansas, census lists Folsom as a lawyer, living with his wife only one household away from the Bridewells. Folsom had apparently recouped some of his losses by this time, for the census lists him as owning five hundred dollars in personal estate and five thousand dollars in real estate.[25]

James Folsom and his wife remained in Camden no more than a year or two. After living briefly in Louisville, Kentucky, the couple settled in 1873 in Dover, New Hampshire, where a number of James's uncles, aunts, and cousins lived. James Folsom apparently pursued a number of different jobs throughout the 1870's. Dover city directories list him as an author in 1874 and a clerk of court in 1876.[26]

By 1889 James Folsom was living at 42 Hammond Street in Boston, Massachusetts, and practicing dentistry. He died at this residence of bronchitis on October 23, 1889 and his body went to Dover, New Hampshire, for burial.[27] It is a real tragedy that the one-time Georgian never completed the record he had started of his native state's participation in the "Revolution of 1861." Additional volumes, especially ones devoted to the Army of Tennessee, would have revealed much that is not known about the role Georgia units played in many of the important battles and campaigns of the Civil War.

Keith S. Bohannon

May 1995

ENDNOTES TO THE INTRODUCTION

[1]Milledgeville (Ga.) *Confederate Union*, March 21, 1865. Original copies of *Heroes and Martyrs* are held at the following institutions: Boston Athenaeum, Duke University, Emory University, Huntington Library, Library of Congress, New York Public Library, the University of Georgia, the University of North Carolina at Chapel Hill, the University of Texas, Wake Forest University, and the Wisconsin Historical Society.

[2]Elizabeth Knowles Folsom, *Genealogy of the Folsom Family* (reprint ed., Baltimore, Md.: Gateway Press, Inc., 1975), pp. 535-36; *Massachusetts Vital Records: Boston Deaths 1849-1890*, microfiche #262.

[3]George White, *Statistics of the State of Georgia* (Savannah, Ga.: W. Thorne Williams, 1849), pp. 614-15.

[4]1850 Wilkinson County, Georgia, Census, p. 385; 1850 Wilkinson County Slave Schedule, p. 927. A fourth and final child of James Sr. and Mary, Richard Arnold, was born in Gordon on July 13, 1851. Richard died in 1875. Folsom, *Genealogy*, p. 536.

[5]1860 Twiggs County, Georgia, Census, pp. 376 and 402.

[6]*Savannah Daily Morning News*, March 4, 1861; 1860 Burke County, Georgia, Census, p. 956; 1860 Burke County, Georgia, Slave Schedule, p. 220.

[7]James M. Folsom to Joseph E. Brown, Gordon, Ga., December 10, 1860, Governor's Incoming Correspondence, RG 1-1-5, Box 30, Loc. 3335-02, Folder marked "James M. Folsom," Georgia State Archives.

[8]James M. Folsom to Joseph E. Brown, Gordon, Ga., April 1, 1861, Governor's Incoming Correspondence, RG 1-1-5, Box 30, Loc. 3335-02, Folder marked "James M. Folsom," Georgia State Archives.

[9]James M. Folsom to Henry C. Wayne, Camp Jackson, Va. June 22, 1861, Telamon Cuyler Collection, Ga. Adjutant General's Papers, Henry C. Wayne, Box 17, Folder 2, Special Collections, University of Georgia.

[10]W. P. Derby and W. C. King, comp., *Campfire Sketches and Battle-field Echoes* (Springfield, Mass.: King, Richardson, & Co., 1889), p. 271.

[11]James M. Folsom Compiled Service Record; Henry W. Thomas, *History of the Doles-Cook Brigade* (Atlanta: Franklin Printing and Publishing Company, 1903), pp. 64-65 and 85.

[12]James M. Folsom to Joseph E. Brown, Doctortown, Ga., August 26, 1862, Governor's Incoming Correspondence, RG 1-1-5, Box 30, Loc. 3335-02, Folder marked "James M. Folsom," Georgia State Archives; Judah P. Benjamin to Joseph E. Brown, Richmond, Va., October 3, 1861, Letters sent by the Confederate Secretary of War, 1861 letterbook, p. 115, National Archives; Special Orders No. 208, Confederate Adjutant and Inspector General's Office, Richmond, November 6, 1861, Telamon Cuyler Collection, MS #1170, Ga. Adjutant General's Papers, Box 17, Folder 2, Special Collections, University of Georgia.

[13]James M. Folsom to Judah P. Benjamin, Gordon, Ga., October 8, 1861, Letters received by the Confederate Secretary of War, National Archives; Judah P. Benjamin to James M. Folsom, Richmond, Va., October 13, 1861, Letters sent by the Confederate Secretary of War, 1861 letterbook, p. 169.

[14]James M. Folsom to George W. Randolph, Doctortown, Ga., April 21, 1862, James M. Folsom Compiled Service Record.

[15]James M. Folsom to Joseph E. Brown, Doctortown, Ga., August 26, 1862, Governor's Incoming Correspondence, RG 1-1-5, Box 30, Loc. 3335-02, folder marked "James M. Folsom," Georgia State Archives.

[16]T. Conn Bryan, *Confederate Georgia* (Athens: University of Georgia Press, 1953), p. 201.

[17]T. Conn Bryan, ed., "Letters of Two Confederate Officers," *Georgia Historical Quarterly* XLVI (1962), p. 194.

[18]Folsom may have taken some of his material out of Georgia newspapers. The vignette on p. 79 of *Heroes and Martyrs* entitled "A Gallant Lieutenant" appears in a slightly different form in the *Macon Telegraph*, June 4, 1864. The latter account had been written by a soldier in the Third Georgia Infantry.

[19]James M. Folsom, *Heroes and Martyrs* (Macon: Burke, Boykin, & Co., 1864), pp. 31, 97 and 104.

[20]*Official Records of the War of the Rebellion*, Series I, Volume 44, pp. 66-67; Joseph T. Maddox, comp., *Wilkinson County, Georgia, Wills and Cemeteries* (n.p., n.d.), p. 98.

[21]*Columbus Daily Sun*, February 17, 1865.

[22]James Folsom went to Virginia to secure his brother's body, burying it in Hollywood Cemetery in Richmond. *Augusta Constitutionalist*, May 14, 1864; *Augusta Constitutionalist*, January 14, 1863; Robert W. Folsom to Maria Folsom, Near Winchester, Va., September 14, 1862, C.S.A. Archives, Officers and soldiers' miscellaneous letters, folder marked "July-December 1862," Duke University.

[23]Milledgeville *Confederate Union*, February 21, 1865; Milledgeville *Southern Recorder*, March 21, 1865. An advertisement for *Heroes and Martyrs* appeared, without editorial comment, in the *Columbus Daily Sun*, February 17, 1865, and the *Lagrange Reporter*, March 3, 1865.

[24]Victor Davidson, "Book Became a Frankenstein," *Atlanta Journal*, March 6, 1932; Wilkinson County, Ga. Superior Court Deed Records, Book A, pp. 785-785; Book B, pp. 136, 208, 226, 228-30 and 244. In 1868, Folsom still owed $50.00 to J. W. Burke & Co., the co-partnership that took over Burke, Boykin, and Co. on February 25, 1865. *Macon Telegraph*, February 28, 1865.

[25]1870 Ouachita County, Arkansas, Census, p. 20; C. A. Bridewell, General and Staff Compiled Service Record; Obituary of C. A. Bridewell in *Hope (Ark) Star*, November 21, 1917.

[26]1874 and 1876 Dover, New Hampshire, City Directories.

[27]Mary M. Folsom survived her husband by less than a year, dying of heart failure in Portland, Maine, on September 7, 1890. James M. Folsom obituary in *Boston Herald*, October 26, 1889; Mary M. Folsom death certificate in City of Portland, Maine, Vital Records, Volume 8, p. 128.

PREFACE

———

The first volume of *Heroes and Martyrs*, &c., which I am herewith presenting to the public, has been written, and the material collected under circumstances of the most unfavorable character, during the hottest portion of one of the most extraordinary campaigns ever fought, on this or any other continent.

The gentlemen who have so kindly assisted me in collecting the material, and whose names I append, were compelled, with perhaps a few exceptions, to lie in the trenches around Petersburg, under an almost constant cannonade, while every instrument of destruction that man's ingenuity could devise, was flying thick and fast around him, and while there wrote out the MSS. from which this volume is compiled.

It was my hope when I commenced my labors, that the larger portion of my work would be filled with incidents of personal heroism; and it is a bitter disappointment to me (owing to the difficulty of obtaining names and incidents,) to present this work to the public, without more of the names of those, to whom it is dedicated, filling its pages.

I have attempted to avoid all superfluity of language, and to render the book perfectly comprehensible to every reader.

The footing up of the losses of the different commands may appear strange to many, especially those whose losses have exceeded their strength, such as the Third and Sixth Regiments. This, however, is explained by the fact, that many of the wounded have been wounded more than once, and that the *real* losses from wounds are those who have been retired or discharged.

I desire to express my thanks to the officers who have so kindly assisted me, and particularly to Colonel Loftin, of the Sixth Georgia, to whose courtesy I am indebted for the facility with which I collected my material while in Virginia. I desire that the following named gentlemen will accept my thanks for their generous assistance, and kind sympathy with my undertaking:

Colonel William Gibson..................................Forty-eighth Georgia Regiment.

Lieutenant-Colonel M. R. Hall......................Forty-eighth Georgia Regiment.
Lieutenant-Colonel Nisbet...Third Georgia Regiment.
Adjutant J. A. Byrd...Sixty-fourth Georgia Regiment.
Major J. D. Frederick..Tenth Georgia Battalion.
Colonel J. N. Ramsey..First Georgia Regiment.
Colonel Neal...Nineteenth Georgia Regiment.
Colonel John T. Loftin...Sixth Georgia Regiment.
Colonel Huggins, and Major Ballenger......Twenty-third Georgia Regiment.
Adjutant T. O. Wicker..................................Twenty-eighth Georgia Regiment.
Sergeant Piser..Twenty-eighth Georgia Regiment.
Major Bassenger...Eighteenth Georgia Battalion.
Sergeant Major Harris..Cutts' Artillery Battalion.
Captain Wofford...Phillips' Legion Cavalry Battalion.
Captain Norwood..Thomas' Brigade.
Adjutant Mark Newman.................................Forty-ninth Georgia Regiment.
Lieutenant-Colonel McCulloh........................Thirty-fifth Georgia Regiment.
Captain T. C. Moore..Fourteenth Georgia Regiment.

In wishing them a happy exemption from the casualties of any future engagement, and the pleasures of a safe and happy return to their homes, when white-robed peace shall again smile upon us, in the enjoyment of our dearest rights, is my heart's sincere feelings.

To the press and public I would say, deal leniently with this work, as it is the labor of a young beginner in the world of literature. If you find, as you no doubt will, abundant food for criticism, then I implore you, for the sake of his motives spare

THE AUTHOR.

CONTENTS

———

TO

The Heroes and Martyrs of Georgia:

WHOSE UNDIMINISHED AND UNWAVERING VALOR HAS LONG BEEN THE PRIDE AND
BOAST OF THEIR NATIVE STATE:

WHOSE SUFFERINGS, PRIVATIONS, WOUNDS, AND DEATHS, HAVE BEEN SO LONG AND
DEEPLY DEPLORED:

WHO, BY THEIR GALLANTRY, HAVE ILLUSTRATED THE CHARACTER OF GEORGIA,
AND
WHO, BY THEIR GLORIOUS DEATHS, HAVE FILLED A NICHE IN THE
TEMPLE OF UNDYING FAME,

THIS WORK IS AFFECTIONATELY DEDICATED BY

THE AUTHOR.

CONDENSED STATISTICAL REPORTS.

NAMES OF REGIMENTS AND BATTALIONS	Strength				Deaths			Losses Otherwise Than by Death					Total of All Losses	Casualties in Battle		
	Volunteers	Recruits	Conscripts	Total	Killed	Died	Total	Wounded	Discharged	Transferred	Deserted	Total		Killed	Wounded	Total
Eighteenth Georgia Regiment	1,070			1,070			200						200			
Sixth Georgia Regiment	841	364	38	1,243	184	180	364	533	142			675	1,039	184	533	717
Nineteenth Georgia Regiment	724	568		1,292	239	244	483	659	189			848	1,331	239	659	898
Twenty-third Georgia Regiment				1,258	184	253	437	630	170			800	1,237	184	630	814
Twenty-eighth Georgia Regiment	794	300	37	1,131	153	175	328	340	164	61	91	656	984	153	340	493
Twenty-seventh Georgia Regiment					153	243	396	280	94			374	770	153	280	433
Third Georgia Regiment	684	467		1,151	104	268	372		174			174	546	104		104
Forty-eighth Georgia Regiment	932	551		1,483	221	272	493	667	342			1,009	1,502	221	667	888
Tenth Georgia Battalion	854	241	33	1,128	189	261	450	358	102		19	479	919	189	358	547
Sixty-fourth Georgia Regiment	346	293	2	641	34	156	190	118	54	4	15	191	381	34	118	152
Phillips' Georgia Legion (Cavalry)	875			875									243			
Cutts' Georgia Artillery Battalion	180	376		556	28	104	132	154	76	43	14	287	419	28	154	182
Eighteenth Georgia Battalion	297	177		456	8	20	28	8	60	48	23	139	167	8	68	76
Forty-ninth Georgia Regiment				1,160	142	289	431	463	194	5	6	668	1,099	142	463	605
Thirty-fifth Georgia Regiment	740	535		1,275	128		128	429				532	660	128	429	557
Fourteenth Georgia Regiment	769	328		1,097	138	212	351	436	178			614	964	138	436	574

GEORGIA VOLUNTEERS

———

The following brief record of the First Georgia Volunteers, from the pen of its Colonel, will be read with interest, as it is the first official history of that regiment, which has come before the public.

The First Regiment of Georgia Volunteers was organized at Macon, on the 3d day of April, 1861, by the election of J. N. Ramsey to the Colonelcy, J. O. A. Clarke to the Lieutenant Colonelcy, and G. Harvey Thompson, Major.

In pursuance of orders from the Governor of Georgia, the regiment departed immediately for Pensacola, Florida, where, under the command of General Bragg, they were for two months employed in preparing the defences for a contemplated attack from the enemy. At the expiration of the two months, the regiment was ordered to report at Richmond, Virginia. On arriving at Richmond, orders were received from the President to repair immediately to Staunton, in the Valley of Virginia. Upon the arrival of the regiment at that point, we were ordered to take up the line of march across the mountains to Laurel Hill, to the support of General Garnett, whose command was threatened by an overpowering force of the enemy, under General G. B. McClellan.

Upon the arrival of the regiment, in June, 1861, it was immediately engaged in fortifying the camp at Laurel Hill, with the few troops under the command of General Garnett; in all not amounting to more than three thousand, at that point.

In a few days, the enemy appeared in large force, in front of our position, and attempted to seize upon the heights, which would, without doubt, have given them complete command over the camp. A sharp combat ensued, in which the First Georgia drove the enemy at the point of the bayonet, from the heights, they leaving many of their dead upon the field. The loss of the First Georgia was very small, not one being killed, one severely, and several slightly wounded. This was the first time the regiment was ever under fire or actively engaged; and their conduct was all their commander could have desired. Skirmishing continued daily for a week, ending almost every evening, with a brisk cannonade by the enemy.

Our position at Rich Mountain having been turned by the enemy, which gave them control of the only road through the mountains by which General Garnett received his supplies, it became necessary to evacuate our position at Laurel Hill. The army, on account of its small numbers, and being cut off from all supplies and support, was now in a very perilous condition. An overwhelming force of the enemy was in our front; a large force which had just taken Rich Mountain, moving in our rear; a large force at New Creek and West Union, in striking distance of the only route by which we could possibly escape; together with the fact that we were already out of provisions, rendered a successful retreat very precarious, and from which nothing but an indomitable resolution to clear ourselves from the toils in which we were ensnared, could ever have relieved us.

The lamented General Garnett, comprehending fully the responsibilities of his position, calmly made his dispositions, and at night-fall, in good order, commenced a retrograde movement in the direction of Beverly; then turning off to the left, pursued the St. George road, in order again to get in communication with his supplies and supports. To accomplish this movement, a long and circuitous route had to be traveled, with impassible mountains on either hand, and an enemy powerful in numbers and munitions of war, was handing upon our rear, and threatening our front at the only point, as before stated, where we could make our escape from this net, whose meshes had entangled us.

On the second day of the retreat, the enemy came upon the rear of our little band of Confederates; the First Georgia covering the retreat. As soon as the enemy conceived a flank movement, the Colonel commanding the First, threw out two companies to the left, who drove them back. A heavy column with artillery, was then discovered advancing upon our troops, who were then filing through Cheat River. In order to protect them, the Colonel of the First Georgia ordered his regiment to face to the right, pass the river, and attack the enemy. Leading four companies across, he ordered fire to open on the advancing column, which was promptly executed, and a galling fire was poured into the advancing foe. Matters upon the left did not progress so well. Six companies were effectually cut off and could not pass, but made their way through the mountains, and joined their comrades after many days of the most intense suffering, in many cases amounting to incipient starvation.

The four companies who were making the desperate stand alluded to above, being almost enveloped by the heavy masses of the enemy, having received no supports, and having entirely despaired of receiving assistance from the six companies who were cut off, and there being but about two hundred of these noble Georgians to contend against the whole Yankee army, who were pouring a hot fire of artillery and musketry into our ranks from every point, were ordered to fall back. In this encounter, the regiment lost twenty men, mostly captured by the enemy.

At the next ford General Garnett made a stand, about a mile from the scene of the conflict above described. At this point, General Garnett lost his life, and Colonel Ramsey took command of the forces by seniority of rank; who, seeing the danger of the situation, ordered a forced march this night, in order to turn the enemy's camp in front, which seemed to be the only chance or hope of escape. The plan was attended with complete success, and the army saved with inconsiderable loss. Too much praise cannot be bestowed upon the loyal citizens of that portion of the Old Dominion, for the timely assistance which they furnished our sick and famishing soldiers, on that toilsome march.

By rapid marches, the army soon arrived at Monterey, and were again moved forward under the command of General Henry R. Jackson of Savannah, to check the enemy's advance on Green Brier River. In an affair on Cheat Mountain, the regiment lost two or three killed, and several wounded; the enemy suffered much more. The main guard of the Yankees were here cut off from under the guns of their fortified camp, and killed, wounded or dispersed by the advance guard of our forces, composed of one hundred men from the First and Twelfth Georgia Regiments.

On the 3d day of October, 1861, the enemy in large force attacked General Jackson, and after a severe contest of eight hours, were driven back with considerable loss. The loss of this regiment amounted to fifty-one killed, wounded and missing.

Lieutenant Colonel Clarke having resigned his commission, an election to fill the vacancy was ordered, and James Thompson was elected. Adjutant J. W. Anderson was elected to the Majority. About the 25th day of December, the regiment was ordered to join the forces of Stonewall Jackson at Winchester, Virginia, and participated in the campaigns of Bath and Romney, one of the most disagreeable of the war, owing to the terrible weather.

The loss of this regiment was considerable, from constant exposure to the many hardships connected with this campaign. The weather was intensely cold, and storms of sleet and rain were numerous.

In March, 1862, the time for which this regiment enlisted expired, and they were mustered out of service. The health of the Colonel, feeble at the beginning of the war, had, in consequence of the exposure and many fatigues he had undergone, almost totally failed, and in consequence, the regiment was never reorganized; but all the members not disabled, after a short respite, were organized into artillery and other companies, and again entered the service. Many were placed in important commands, which they now hold in the Confederate army; and not a few have nobly fallen on the many gory battle-fields of this revolution.

Composed of intelligent patriots, brave and self-sacrificing heroes, they bore patiently the severe trials and sufferings through which they passed. Their commander found it necessary only to appeal to their sense of duty, to enforce discipline; and in no case, during their term of service, was any officer court-martialed for failure to discharge his duty, or for conduct unbecoming an officer or a gentleman. The severest punishment inflicted upon a private, was confinement in the guard tent for a few days.

The total losses of the regiment from all causes, was about two hundred, mostly from sickness and unavoidable exposure.

The above history of the first regiment Georgia sent into the field, is incomplete, as all statistical records are lost, and at this late day, many of the most interesting facts and much important matter connected with the regiment, cannot be obtained.

Since the above was written, I have received the following statement of the original organization of the First Georgia Regiment:—

Company A, Newnan Guards, Coweta County, Captain G. M. Harvey.

Company B, Southern Guards, Muscogee County, Captain F. Wilkins.

Company C, Southern Rights Guards, Houston County, Captain J. A. Houser.

Company D, Oglethorpe Light Infantry, Richmond County, Captain — Adams.

Company E, Washington Rifles, Washington County, Captain S. A. H. Jones.

Company F, Gate City Guards, Fulton County, Captain W. Ezzard.

Company G, Quitman Guards, Monroe County, Captain J. S. Pinckard.

Company H, Dahlonega Volunteers, Lumpkin County, Captain T. B. Cabiness.

Company I, Bainbridge Independent Volunteers, Decatur County, Captain
      J. W. Evans.
Company K, Walker Light Infantry, Richmond County, Captain — Crump.
      Lieutenant James Anderson, of Company A, *Adjutant.*
      Henry Welch, of Company A, *Sergeant Major.*
      P. D. B. Culler, of Perry, Georgia, *Surgeon.*
      [No Assistant Surgeon.]
      Lieutenant Atkinson, of Columbus, *Quartermaster.*
      Captain George Dunn, of Forsyth, *Quartermaster.*
      Captain G. Cunningham, *Commissary.*

EIGHTEENTH REGIMENT

GEORGIA VOLUNTEERS

STATISTICAL REPORT OF EIGHTEENTH GEORGIA VOLUNTEERS.

Number of men originally enlisted, ...   841
Number of recruits, ...   364
Number of conscripts, ...   38
        Total strength of regiment: 1243

CASUALTIES IN DIFFERENT ENGAGEMENTS.

		Killed.	*Wounded.*
May 7th..................1862,	Eltham's Landing,		
May 31st..................1862,	Seven Pines,		3
June 27th................1862,	Gaines' Farm,	37	106
July 2d.....................1862,	Malvern Hill,		
	Freeman's Ford,		
August 29th............1862,	Thoroughfare Gap,		
August 30th............1862,	Manassas, Number 2,	37	37
September 14th.....1862,	Boonsboro Gap,		1
September 17th.....1862,	Sharpsburg,	27	63
December 13th......1862,	Fredericksburg,	14	30
May 3d....................1863,	Chancellorsville,	21	80
July 2d.....................1863,	Gettysburg,	31	9
	Chester Gap,		
September..............1863,	Chattanooga,		3
November 29th......1863,	Knoxville,	15	23
December 13th......1863,	Bean Station,		1

May 6th.................1864,	Wilderness,	7	37
May 10, 11, & 12...1864,	Spottsylvania Court House,	10	30
June 1st..................1864,	Coal Harbor,	4	25
July 29th................1864,	Deep Bottom,		
	TOTAL,	184	533

Number of men died of wounds and disease, ...   180
Number of men discharged, ...   142

RECAPITULATION.

Killed, ...	184
Wounded, ...	533
Died, ...	180
Discharged	142
TOTAL,	1039

By the foregoing recapitulation and statistical report, it will be seen that this regiment has been actively engaged in twenty battles, in fifteen of which it suffered more or less.

The total loss, counting the wounded men, many of whom are of course still in the regiment, amounts to one thousand and thirty-nine men. This is, however, only a temporary loss. The real loss of the regiment is as follows:–

Killed, ...	184
Died, ...	180
Discharged, ...	142
Amounting to, ...	506 men.

The Eighteenth Georgia Regiment was organized at Camp Brown, Cobb County, Georgia, on the 22d day of April, 1861, under a special act of the Georgia Legislature, and formed the First Regiment, Fourth Brigade, State Troops, under the following named field officers: Colonel W. T. Wofford, of Cassville, Cass County; Lieutenant Colonel S. Z. Ruff, of the Georgia Military Institute,

Marietta, Cobb County; Major Jefferson Johnson, Floyd County; Adjutant John C. Griffin, Marietta, Cobb County.

The changes in the field officers are as follows: Adjutant J. C. Griffin elected Major, April 7th, 1862, to succeed Major Johnson, resigned. Colonel Wofford was appointed Brigadier General, January 1st, 1863, successor to General T. R. R. Cobb, killed December 13th, 1862. Lieutenant A. H. Patton promoted Adjutant, April 7th, 1862, successor to Adjutant Griffin, promoted Major. Lieutenant Colonel Ruff promoted to the Colonelcy, January 1st, 1863, successor to Colonel Wofford, promoted Brigadier.

Captain J. A. Stewart promoted to Major, successor to Major John C. Griffin, appointed Commissary of Subsistence. Captain Joseph Armstrong appointed Colonel, January 6th, 1864, successor to Colonel Ruff, killed November 29th, 1863. Captain F. M. Ford appointed Lieutenant Colonel, March 25th, 1864, successor to Lieutenant Colonel Ruff. Captain W. G. Calahan appointed Major, January 6th, successor to Major Stewart, resigned. Sergeant E. N. Everett appointed Adjutant, successor to Adjutant Patton, who was appointed Captain and Assistant Adjutant General on General Wofford's staff.

The brigade was organized – day of –, –, and transferred to Camp McDonald, Cobb County, Georgia. After nearly two months of preparatory drilling at the latter place, the brigade (the Fourth, State Troops,) was broken up, and the regiments and battalions composing it were ordered to report to Richmond, having been transferred to the service of the Confederate States.

The regiment left Camp McDonald on the 2d day of August, 1861, and arrived at Richmond on the 7th. During the greater portion of the time they were in Richmond, they were on duty guarding the prisoners captured in the first battle of Manassas. On the 26th of October, the regiment having been relieved from this duty by the Second Florida Regiment, received orders to report to Goldsboro, North Carolina, for garrison duty. They remained here about two weeks, when they received orders to report back to Richmond. On the 18th, they departed for the Potomac, and were attached to the Texas brigade then commanded by General Wigfall, and were stationed in the vicinity of Dumfries. Here they remained all winter, doing picket and other duties. On the 8th of March, 1862, the Eighteenth left camp on the Potomac, and entered upon the campaign of that year with the Army of Northern Virginia.

The brigade, at this time, was under the command of Brigadier General Hood, General Wigfall having resigned. The brigade marched from Dumfries to Yorktown, which being the first march of the regiment, and the men being unaccustomed to the hardships of a long march, suffered greatly from the exposure and severities of the march. They were afterwards detailed to guard the right flank of the army, on its retreat from Yorktown. On the seventh of May, the enemy in considerable force, attacked the right flank of General Johnson's army, and were repulsed by the brigade near Eltham's Landing, the Eighteenth Georgia bearing a conspicuous part in the engagement. On the 31st of May and the 1st of June, the regiment participated in the battle of Seven Pines, sustaining a loss of three men wounded. The regiment was afterward kept in the Chickahominy Swamp, doing picket duty, and throwing up fortifications, &c., until the 12th of June, when they were transported to Staunton, to reinforce General Stonewall Jackson; at which point they arrived on the 18th; and on the 19th left Staunton, and were transported to Frederick's Hall, remaining there for two days to prepare for the great work anticipated by that far-seeing chieftain, General Jackson.

On the 26th, the regiment arrived in front of Richmond, opposite Mechanicsville, and at four o'clock in the evening, on the 27th of June, they went into the battle of Gaines' Farm, charging the enemy's batteries, placed in position under the immediate supervision of General McClellan himself, and said by him to be impregnable; but the intrepid spirits composing the Texas brigade, needed only the command of *onward*, to drive the vandals from their guns, and turn them upon the retreating foe. The battle closed about nine o'clock in the evening, the whole country being covered with the victims of the horrid strife.

The Eighteenth Georgia in this engagement, captured nine splendid brass pieces of artillery, with a loss to the regiment of thirty-seven killed, and one hundred and six wounded. They remained on the field the remainder of the night. The 28th was spent in burying the dead, and caring for the wounded. On the 29th, they took up the line of march in pursuit of McClellan's retreating and badly whipped forces. On the 31st, the regiment received a heavy shelling at White Oak Swamp, but sustained no loss. On the 1st of July, it took an active part in the battle of Malvern Hill. The casualties in this fight were three killed and seven wounded. On the 4th, the regiment marched to Charles City Court House. The regiment was very much fatigued, but after remaining at the latter place four days, were ready and willing to perform any duty which might have been assigned it.

On the 8th, the regiment marched for Richmond, where it arrived on the 10th. Here it went into camp, where it quietly remained until the 7th of August, when, in response to the command of *forward*, it marched to the plains of Manassas, where it arrived on the 29th of August, having undergone many hardships and privations, being frequently compelled to subsist on green corn, as it was impossible to obtain any other kind of food. The regiment during this march, was engaged in two different encounters with the enemy, the first at Freeman's Ford, and the second at Thoroughfare Gap.

At six o'clock in the evening of the 29th of August, the regiment engaged the enemy in a hand to hand encounter. After two hours hard fighting, they succeeded in repulsing the enemy, with the following result: A large number of prisoners were taken. Private T. H. Northcutt of Company A, captured one stand of colors belonging to the Twenty-fourth New York Regiment. On the 30th, the regiment participated in the second battle of Manassas, completely routing the enemy, killing the greater portion of the Fifth and Tenth New York Zouave Regiments, and capturing a battery of four guns.

During the heat of the engagement, Private William Kay succeeded in capturing the colors of the Tenth New York Regiment. The casualties during this terrific battle in the old Eighteenth, amounted to thirty-seven killed and eighty-seven wounded.

August 31st was spent in burying the dead and attending to the wounded. The regiment left during the latter date, and by severe marching arrived at the Potomac on the 5th day of September, crossed and marched to Frederick City, Maryland, where it remained and rested three days. On the 14th of September a portion of the army were hotly engaged at Boonsborough Mountain. Hood's Brigade, by a forced march, arrived in time to take a part in the engagement. The Eighteenth Georgia in this fight lost but one wounded. On the 17th of September the regiment was engaged in the battle of Sharpsburg, and from five o'clock in the morning until late in the evening, bore a prominent part in that bloody strife, losing (27) twenty-seven killed and (63) sixty-three wounded. During the night of the 18th the regiment recrossed the Potomac at Shepherdstown, and were there compelled to assist the teamsters in gaining the heights on the south bank of the river, the mud being too deep for the half-worn down animals to drag their loads through, which consisted of principally army stores, collected from the enemy while in Maryland and Pennsylvania. The regiment encamped for the remainder of the night at Martinsburg, and after a week of much needed rest, again took up the line of march for Winchester, where it went into camp on the 29th, remaining there for one month. At this point the regiment received a new supply of clothing, of which they stood greatly in need, particularly of shoes. Many of the poor Georgia boys had marched mile after mile and fought several battles with their feet bare, and bleeding at almost every step. On the 29th of October the regiment again struck camp and marched for Culpepper, arriving there on the 1st day of November, and on the 20th of the same month marched in Fredericksburg, at which place it arrived and went into camp on the 28th. Under an order from the War Department, the regiment was transferred from General Hood's Texas Brigade to General Cobb's Georgia Brigade. This change, at the time, was not much relished by the majority of the regiment, who were not pleased at the idea of leaving their old and tried companions in arms, the Texans; but their new commander, the lamented Cobb, soon won their confidence and admiration by his urbanity and zeal for their welfare, together with the many soldierly qualities which had already marked him out for high preferment in the military line, and which were unfortunately too soon thereafter lost to his brigade and country.

On December 13th, together with the remainder of Cobb's Brigade, the regiment went into the battle of Fredericksburg, in which engagement it sustained very nobly its former dearly bought reputation. It was upon this day that the brigade lost its gallant leader, General Cobb, who fell while among his noble band of Georgians, speaking words of encouragement, and cheering them with his presence.

In this engagement, one of the severest of the war, the Eighteenth killed, in all probability, one half its number – itself sustaining a loss of fourteen killed and thirty wounded.

The regiment remained in camp after the battle of Fredericksburg until the night of the 20th of April, when it marched up to Chancellorsville, where it lay in line of battle until the 3d of May, when the great contest began. The regiment was very hotly engaged for one hour and twenty-five minutes, confronting the formidable works of the enemy, and sustaining a loss of twenty-one killed and eighty-six wounded. On May 4th, an advance was made upon the enemy and he was driven toward Banksford, losing a great many prisoners. On the 1st of June the regiment marched for Culpepper Court House, where it arrived after two days severe marching. On the 16th, it marched from Culpepper by way of Woodsville, Sperryville, Little Washington, to Parria, and crossed the Shenandoah River. On the 21st, recrossed the river at Ashby's Gap, and lay in line of battle as support to cavalry. On the 22d, it crossed back to same camp. On the 24th, marched by way of Millwood, Berryville, Summer Point, Smythville and Darksville, to Martinsburg; crossed the Potomac, on the 26th, at Williamsport, and marched by way of Hagerstown, Middleburg, Green Castle, Chambersburg and Cashtown, to Gettysburg, where it arrived on the 31st.

The troops suffered very severely on this march from the excessive heat; so great was it indeed that as many as one hundred cases of sun-stroke occurred in the division during one day. On the 2d day of July the regiment was engaged in the battle of Gettysburg, driving the enemy for over a mile, and resting on the field during the night. The casualties were nine killed and thirty-one wounded. On the night of the 4th, marched by way of Fairfield and Waterloo, to Hagerstown, remaining at the latter place until the 14th of August, awaiting an attack from the enemy. At that time the regiment recrossed the Potomac at Williamsport, marched to Bunker Hill; from thence to Culpepper Court House, where it arrived on the 24th instant. While on the march from Bunker Hill to Culpepper, the regiment was engaged in dislodging a body of the enemy's cavalry, sustaining no loss whatever.

General Longstreet's Corps being selected by General Lee to reinforce General Bragg, in the West, the regiment accordingly, on the 9th of September, was placed on the cars at Hanover Junction, and were, without delay, transported to Chickamauga, Georgia, where it arrived on the 19th, but did not participate in the battle of that name, as the brigade could not get up to the scene of action in time. After some days spent in skirmishing with the enemy, in which the regiment lost altogether three men wounded, it was again, on the 5th of October, transported by railroad, by way of Cleveland, Charlestown and Athens, to Sweet Water, Tennessee. On the 12th, it marched from Sweet Water, by way of Philadelphia, Morganton, Lowdon, Lenoir Station, to Campbell's Station, where it arrived on the 17th and took part in a heavy skirmish with the enemy, but sustained no loss of life. On the 18th, marched within two miles of Knoxville. Heavy skirmishing was inaugurated and continued every day until the 29th instant, when the Eighteenth participated in the celebrated charge of McLaws' Division on Fort Lowdon, in which the regiment sustained one of the most irreparable losses which could have befallen it, viz: the loss of its gallant leader, Colonel S. Z. Ruff. Each member of the regiment, with perhaps a very few exceptions, mourned the loss of their Colonel as they would the loss of a father or a brother. Having been led by him in every engagement, save two or three, they had become ardently attached to him, always feeling that all was right with the Eighteenth Georgia, at least, when Colonel Ruff was in command. All honor to his name. The Colonel was commanding Wofford's Brigade when he received the shot that ended his earthly career. He received his mortal wound while endeavoring to scale the walls of the fort. His name will long occupy a place in the memories of the members of the regiment, who he had so long commanded. May he rest in peace. During this engagement, the regiment lost fifteen killed, and twenty-three wounded. On the night of the 4th of December, the regiment marched by way of Rutledge and Moorsburg, to Bean Station, where, on the 13th, it participated in a small skirmish with the enemy; remaining at the latter place until the 20th, when it marched across the Holston river to Russelville, and received orders to build winter quarters. The men since the departure of the regiment from before Chattanooga, and during the hard marching and fighting up to the time of their arrival at Russelville, had suffered severely for clothing, especially for shoes and blankets, and the weather being extremely cold in that region, adding to which the continued snow and rain, showed many cases of real misery; but the spirits of these noble sons of the Empire State rose proudly above all physical suffering, and but few murmurs were ever heard.

The men went to work with a will, and soon had some very comfortable cabins erected, just in time for the Christmas holidays, and it is almost needless to add that this mode of living was duly appreciated by all.

The regiment remained in quarters until the 11th of February, when it moved to New Market, when they again built winter quarters, and there remained until the 22d, when they marched to Greenville, remaining there until the 28th of March, when they again took the road marching for Bristol, where they arrived on the 31st.

The regiment while encamped at Greenville, *re-enlisted unanimously for the war.* On the 10th of April, the regiment was placed on board the cars, and transported to Charlottesville, Virginia. From thence they marched to Gordonsville, and from thence to the battle ground of the Wilderness; arriving there just in time by a forced march, to participate in the memorable battle fought on the 6th of May. The regiment with the remainder of Wofford's Brigade, went into the fight at eight o'clock in the morning, and very soon the command *forward*, was given, and in a few moments, the leaden messengers of death might be heard whistling through the ranks. The enemy were stubborn, and refused to give an inch of ground. Just at this time, General Wofford asked and obtained permission to make a flank movement on the enemy's left, which was attended with the most signal and triumphant success. Done as it was, with great promptness and celerity of movement, it caused the utter rout of the enemy all along his front, thereby turning the tide of battle in favor of General Lee.

General Wofford merits a great deal of credit for the masterly manner in which this move was planned and carried into execution. The regiment lost in this engagement, seven killed and thirty-seven wounded. On the night of the 7th of May, the regiment marched for Spottsylvania Court House, arriving there at eleven o'clock, on the morning of the 8th. Although the men were completely exhausted, they were immediately put into position in the lines, and on the 12th, participated in the battle known, as the Horse Shoe, during which the Eighteenth charged the enemy, and retook a portion of the fortifications. The regiment lost in this battle, ten men killed and thirty wounded. After some fighting and marching, the regiment reached Coal Harbor, and there on the 1st of June, was engaged in the battle known by that name, losing four men killed and twenty-five wounded.

Among the historical regiments of Georgia proudly stands the battle-scarred Eighteenth. Though no minstrel has tuned his harp to sing the praises, though not seeking, and therefore not obtaining a newspaper reputation, this noble regiment has gained a name which will live through all future time; in the memory of those who have so closely watched its career of glory. Twenty times has its battle flag, the glorious Cross of the Confederacy, been observed with its fiery folds flashing brightly over as many gory fields. The soil of Virginia has "drank, deeply drank" the life blood of many of these noble Georgians, as half clad and freezing, with feet bare and bleeding at every step, they plunged, with the startling, piercing, enthusiastic yell of the Southern soldiery, into the midst of the fight, driving in utter rout, the well dressed Federals before them. The sufferings of our forefathers at the historic Valley Forge, can scarce compare with the sufferings of the members of this and other regiments, but amid all their privations, when hunger with its gnawing pangs attacked them, and they suffering with a hundred discomforts, at the call of their leader, they would spring to their arms, and rush into the midst of the fray, caring for nought but for victory to again perch upon their banners.

GEORGIA VOLUNTEERS

The Sixth Georgia was organized at Atlanta, Georgia, on the 27th day of May, 1861, and was composed of the following companies:

Company A–Hancock County   Captain W. M. Arnold, Commanding.
Company B–Dade County   Captain John G. Hannah, Commanding.
Company C–Houston County   Captain C. D. Anderson, Commanding.
Company D–Butts County   Captain John W. Newton, Commanding.
Company E–Crawford County   Captain Wilde C. Cleveland, Commanding.
Company F–Mitchell County   Captain E. H. Shackleford, Commanding.
Company G–Taylor County   Captain John T. Griffin, Commanding.
Company H–Baker County   Captain A. H. Colquitt, Commanding.
Company I–Twiggs County   Captain John A. Barclay, Commanding.
Company K–Oglethorpe County Captain John T. Loftin, Commanding.

STATISTICAL REPORT.

Number of men originally enlisted, ...   24
Number of recruits and conscripts, ...   <u>568</u>
       Total,   1292

LOSSES.

Killed in action, ...   288
Wounded, ...   639
Died of disease, ...   244

Discharged, ...	189
Which shows a loss by death of, ...	482
To which add discharged, ...	189
Making a total loss to the regiment of, ...	1039

    This regiment was mustered into service by Major Elzey, and was the first from the State of Georgia,* and I believe from the Confederacy, enlisted for the war. Captain A. H. Colquitt was elected Colonel; Captain J. M. Newton, Lieutenant Colonel, and Philemon Tracy, of Bibb, Major. Private W. F. Plane was elected Captain of Company H, and First Lieutenant Lewis J. Dupree was promoted Captain of Company D.

    The regiment at once proceeded to Richmond, Virginia, and at that place received orders to report immediately to Colonel J. B. Magruder, at Yorktown, Virginia.

    On the 4th of June, 1861, six days before the battle of Bethel, we reached Yorktown. Though within hearing of the guns, we did not participate in the first infantry engagement of the war. While anxiously awaiting orders to join our comrades on the field, intelligence reached us that our arms were victorious, and that Butler was retreating to his stronghold at Fortress Monroe. We were stationed at Yorktown from June 4th, 1861, until 3d of May, 1862. During these eleven months, with the exception of a slight skirmish, the Sixth Georgia did no fighting; but by thorough drilling, and those long and repeated marches by which General Magruder threatened first one point and then another, and thus, by artful and rapid movements with an inconsiderable force, kept a large and formidable army inside their fortifications, the regiment was preparing for the arduous duties and brilliant achievements of the future. While at Yorktown we lost one hundred and twenty-five men; and very often by far the greater portion of the regiment was prostrated by sickness. Many of the diseases were incident to, and inseparable from, camp life, and the great and sudden change in the mode of living; but in my judgment, the greater part had their origin in defective policing of the camp. Those who thus died, far from their kindred and their homes, deserve not less the love and admiration of their country, than those who fell upon the field of battle. Hundreds of our sick were removed

---

  * I shall give the history of this regiment in the language of Colonel Loftin, its commander.

to Gloucester county, on the opposite side of the York; and through the unprecedented attention of her worthy citizens, the lives of many were saved. Their fathers, mothers, brothers and sisters could not have treated them with greater kindness. The names of Dr. Jones and his estimable wife, Mr. and Mrs. Baytop, Mr. and Mrs. Catlett, Mr. and Mrs. Stevens, and Mr. and Mrs. Stubbs, and others, will be cherished in affectionate remembrance as long as a single member of the Sixth Georgia survives. They fully sustained the far-famed reputation of the Old Dominion for hospitality. In the late fiery ordeal through which the citizens of Gloucester have passed, from Yankee invasion, she has had the cordial sympathy of the members of the Sixth Georgia, and it has been a common remark in the regiment, that there are no people in the defence of whose homes and firesides its members would sooner pour out their blood. On the 5th of April, General McClellan, with more than one hundred thousand men, was brought to a halt in front of the work at Yorktown, by the brave and dauntless little army of General Magruder, numbering not more than nine thousand. On the 16th, the Sixth Georgia was, for the first time, under fire, having been thrown out as skirmishers, a few hundred yards in advance of the works, to discover the precise position of the enemy. Here we had three men wounded, Dr. James M. Montgomery, of Company H, being one of them, and the first man ever wounded in the regiment. After the arrival of General Johnson's army at Yorktown, we were temporarily attached to a brigade commanded by Brigadier General Gabriel J. Rains, of torpedo notoriety, and placed in the Division of General D. H. Hill. On the 3d of May, with General Johnson's army, we evacuated Yorktown and commenced the retreat, which after great suffering and privation, ended in the works around Richmond. At no time during the war has the Sixth Georgia suffered as it did on this retreat. At the battle of Williamsburg, though on the field we did not engage the enemy. We reached Richmond, broken down and exhausted, as did the entire army. Fortunately for the cause of the Confederacy, General McClellan gave time for rest and to revive the broken spirits of his troops: and in a few weeks they were ready and anxious to drive back the invaders.

In the battle of Seven Pines, on the 31st of May, the regiment was for the first time, heavily engaged with the enemy. The right companies sustained very heavy loss in this action. We lost besides many other gallant soldiers, Adjutant James Reid, a young man of the finest promise, an elegant scholar, a brave soldier, and one who had endeared himself to the entire regiment, by his gentlemanly deportment, unostentatious manners, and kind and noble heart. This is the only battle in which Colonel Colquitt commanded the regiment, as shortly afterward he was placed in command of the brigade, and subsequently received, after the battle of Sharpsburg, the well merited appointment of Brigadier General. From the battle of Seven Pines, until the 26th of June, the regiment was quietly encamped on the Williamsburg road, about four miles from Richmond; at which time, under the command of Lieutenant Colonel J. M. Newton, it broke up camp, preparatory for the great battles around Richmond. By ten o'clock, A.M., of the 26th of Junes, after a march of about ten miles, we halted in sight of Mechanicsville, and impatiently listened for the guns, that were to inaugurate the battles upon which the fate of Richmond depended.

About four P.M., the battle commenced, but it was not until dark, that our front was cleared at Meadow Bridge, by the brave command of General A. P. Hill, and we crossed over and rested for the night on the field of battle, from which the enemy had been driven. They had, however, retreated but a short distance, and at daylight, could be seen in great force, and strongly fortified on the road about one mile from Mechanicsville. While expecting orders to move forward and charge the enemy, General Jackson's columns moved upon his right flank, and forced him to abandon his strong position, with but slight loss on our part. Though not engaged, we had a few casualties in the Sixth.

The road being cleared, we at once moved on towards the bloody field of Cold Harbor, under a burning sun. We marched rapidly, and reached the battle-field about one o'clock in the afternoon. Under a hot fire from the batteries on the adjacent hills, we were thrown first on one part of the lines, and then on the other, as the enemy seemed to be concentrating upon one or the other points. At last we were ordered forward and soon met the foe. With a shout, our boys charged, and the enemy gave way until reinforced by a second line of battle, when we were halted, and with our thinned ranks, fought most desperately for more than two hours. Just at this time, reinforcements were sent to our relief, and mistaking us for the enemy, poured a desperate volley into our rear. Even under the concentrated fire from friend and foe, our shattered ranks stood unbroken. The reinforcements swept by, driving the enemy before them. Darkness coming on, under order, we retired a few hundred yards to the rear, and slept upon our arms. Our loss in this battle was exceedingly heavy; the casualties numbered more than two hundred killed and wounded, being fully half the number carried into action.

Next morning, our line was as distinctly marked by the dead, as it was the evening before, by the living. For three days, we remained near Cold Harbor, and on the third day, crossed McClellan's Bridge, and hastened on, until checked by the enemy's batteries at White Oak Swamp. At this place, a heavy artillery duel took place, which lasted until night, with but little loss on our side. Next morning the enemy were gone. Being the 1st day of July, 1862, we moved forward to the disastrous field of Malvern Hill, where our gallant soldiers were expected to accomplish what Napoleon with his victorious legions would hardly have attempted.

About six o'clock in the afternoon, the Sixth Georgia went into the fight; and as we were moved forward, the regiment was detached from the brigade, by order of General D. H. Hill, and filing to the right, formed line of battle under a murderous fire of shell, grape, canister, and minnie balls. The regiment advanced without any support, right and left, as far as could be seen, through an open field, to within good range, and opened fire upon the enemy, under certainly the most terrific fire that ever shook the hills of Virginia. In a few moments, our regiment to the last man, would have been swept down, when fortunately for us, a brigade of another division, moved up to our right, and drew the destructive fire upon themselves. At each volley they fell by scores, and large gaps were made in their ranks. The bravest men the world has ever seen, could not have accomplished the task before them; and the brigade broke in confusion, and our little band once more stood alone. But before the guns were turned upon us, orders came to fall back, and in some confusion, the regiment did so. Throughout this battle, our worthy Chaplain, Alexander M. Thigpen, bore himself most gallantly, evincing a courage and patriotism in the cause of the Confederacy, only surpassed by his zeal and devotion in the cause of his Master. On this day many others distinguished themselves by their coolness and courage, but the list is too long to enumerate.

The regiment was encamped near Richmond until the 8th day of August, 1862; when with a portion of General D. H. Hill's Division, it moved, under command of General Ripley, to Orange Court House, and after remaining at this place a few days, marched to Manassas, reaching there the day after the battle in which the great braggart, Pope, was so severely handled.

About September 2d, we rejoined the main army near Centreville, marching by way of Leesburg, to Frederick, Maryland, and reaching that place on the 6th. The army only remained four days at Frederick City, at the expiration of which time, General D. H.

Hill's Division moved to South Mountain or Boonsboro. In the battle which took place here on the 14th, General D. H. Hill's Division alone, for many hours, held at least *seventy thousand* of the Federal troops at bay. The Sixth Georgia was very slightly engaged, the enemy not attempting to pass our immediate front, holding as we did, a very strong position in a dense woods, in a gorge of a mountain. On the night of the 14th, our forces fell back to Sharpsburg; and on the 17th of September, fought one of the bloodiest battles of the war.

The battle opened at early dawn, and in a few moments, the Sixth Georgia was in the hottest of the fight. For several hours, the regiment fought as bravely as ever men fought, and held their ground until none were left to hold it. Our loss on this field was almost incredible. We went into the battle with not more than two hundred and fifty men; and of this number, eighty-one were left dead on the field, one hundred and fifteen were wounded, and about thirty taken prisoners. Here fell Lieutenant Colonel Newton, a good man, a most excellent soldier. Without military education, his aptitude for everything pertaining to the military, his dignity of character, his iron will, his stern sense of justice, made him not only an efficient, but a popular officer. He possessed that rare faculty, the result of a happy combination of moral and mental traits, that enabled him to exact implicit obedience to every order, and at the same time, to win the respect and affection of his soldiers. Here, too, fell the chivalric, elegant and gifted Major Phil Tracy. His eloquence had done no little to rouse the people of the state to secession. Though physical infirmities rendered him unfit for active field service, he was among the first to step forward and offer his life in defence of his country. All vicissitudes of time, whether of prosperity or adversity, had left his pure heart as guileless as a child's. He was magnanimous, and liberal to a fault, and all who knew him loved him. He fell universally mourned by the whole regiment; for all felt that a generous, brave and patriotic heart had ceased to beat.

If space permitted, there are others to whom I would gladly refer, and who are worthy of any tribute which could be paid to their memories. Plane, Hannah, Jordan, McCants, Bartlett, Floyd, Wimberly and Reid, all sleep in glory, sacrificed upon the hard fought field of Sharpsburg. After this battle, Captain Loftin was promoted to the position of Colonel, Captain Cleveland to Lieutenant Colonel, and Captain Anderson to the rank of Major. About this time the brigade, commanded by Brigadier General Colquitt, was composed of the following regiments: Sixth, Twenty-third, Twenty-seventh, and Twenty-eighth Georgia, and the Thirteenth Alabama. Soon after, the

Thirteenth Alabama was exchanged for the Nineteenth Georgia Regiment.

On the 19th of September, the regiment with the entire army recrossed the Potomac, and encamped in the vicinity of Winchester, until about the 25th of October; at which time it marched to Charlestown, and aided in tearing up the Winchester and Harper's Ferry railroad. On the morning of the 3d of November, we waded the Shenandoah, and halted for a few days at Paris Gap. On the 5th marched to Front Royal; recrossed the Shenandoah on the night of the 7th, in a snow storm; and arrived at Strasburg on the 11th of November. The regiment was employed a few days in tearing up the Manassas Gap railroad, and leaving on the 16th, marched to Gordonsville, by way of New Market, which place we reached on the 21st. About the 25th of November we reached Port Royal, and were inactive until the 13th of December, on which day we participated in the first battle of Fredericksburg. In this battle the regiment lost but few men.

We spent the winter on the Rappahannock, about four miles from the ill-fated city of Fredericksburg. The time was spent in drilling, and fully equipping the troops for the coming campaign. General Lee neglected nothing that was conducive to the thorough discipline and organization of the army. Five out of every twenty days, were spent as pickets on the banks of the Rappahannock, opposite the splendid residence of Mr. Seddon, brother to the present Secretary of War, which has recently been burned to the ground, by order of Butler, the Beast. On the 29th day of April, 1863, broke up camps and marched to Fredericksburg. Early on the morning of May 2d, we commenced under General Stonewall Jackson, the flank movement to the enemy's right, which proved so disastrous to them, and sent the Eleventh Corps of General Hooker with several others, panic-stricken to the bank of the river. Attached to General Jackson's Corps, General Colquitt's Brigade moved first, left in front, which threw the Sixth Georgia at the head of the brigade. General Jackson rode at the head of the column and personally superintended everything. Everything which was done to facilitate the movements of the corps, was done under his immediate eye. He would direct us to the best place for making the most insignificant crossing, and would not leave until it was completed. No doubt, this personal attention to everything concerning his corps, had much to do with his wonderful success.

About an hour by sun, the corps had formed line of battle at what is called the Wilderness, and on the right flank of General

Hooker's army. The order forward was given, and through the thick undergrowth which was almost impassable, with shouts and yells, the corps rushed on. The pickets were encountered, and gave way at once. The Yankee line of battle stood but little longer than the pickets; and in a few moments, the whole mass was flying in the utmost dismay and confusion. The enemy were preparing for supper, and were not in the least expecting an attack; and in my opinion, darkness alone saved the army of General Hooker from utter destruction. All night we remained in line of battle. About ten o'clock, it began to be whispered from one to another, that General Jackson was mortally wounded; and though every effort was made to conceal the fact from the corps, there were few who by morning, had not learned the sad intelligence.

Another secret of the success of this great and good man, was that he always attacked the enemy when and where he least expected an attack. I do not mean any imputation upon those who assumed the command after General Jackson left the field, but it was apparent to the most superficial observer, that the corps did not move with the same buoyant, proud step, with the same air of confidence and triumph, as when their great leader was at the head of the column, and when they could now and then catch a gleam of his eagle eye.

The next day the regiment fought near the Chancellorsville house, going into the fight about ten o'clock, and driving the enemy with little difficulty about a mile. We held their line until the fighting ceased, and about four o'clock retired to the rear. In the two battles of the Wilderness and Chancellorsville, the loss of the regiment was not heavy. The casualties in both amounted to not more than fifty killed and wounded. Hooker, whipped and baffled by General Lee, recrossed the Rappahannock; and on the 6th of May the regiment rested in its old camp. Here it remained until about the 20th of the same month, when it was ordered to Kingston, North Carolina; at which point it was stationed until the 2d of July, when it was ordered to Richmond, and on the 9th started for Charleston, South Carolina. We arrived at Charleston on the 13th, and had a slight skirmish on James Island on the 16th. While at Charleston, from the 13th of July until February 9th, 1864, the regiment did much duty, bearing its full share of all the dangerous and arduous work at Battery Wagner and Fort Sumter. At both places we lost some of our best soldiers.

On the 20th of January, 1864, Lieutenant Colonel Anderson having resigned, Major Arnold was promoted to the rank of Lieutenant Colonel, having previously been appointed Major on the resignation of Lieutenant Colonel Cleveland, June 16th, 1863. On the 9th of February the regiment, in advance of the brigade, left Charleston for Savannah, Georgia, and on the next day received orders to report to General Finnegan, at Lake City, Florida, which place we reached on the 14th of February. On the 17th we rejoined the brigade at Olustee, and on the 20th engaged in the battle of Ocean Pond. In this engagement the regiment was detached from the brigade, and fought on the extreme left of the line of battle.

Whether we consider the great disparity of numbers, or the result attained, this was one of the finest victories of the war. With not more than (3500) thirty-five hundred men, we whipped and completely routed nearly three times that number. The battle lasted for four hours; and at one time, for at least half an hour, the regiment was without ammunition, except as it was obtained from the cartridge boxes of the killed and wounded. Under a heavy fire the regiment stood its ground, not giving an inch. When almost the last round of ammunition was expended, and the bravest began to despair, a supply of ammunition was received. About this time a portion of Colquitt's Brigade, that had been held in reserve, came up, and our entire line pressed forward with a shout. The enemy gave way before our invincible column, and in a few moments was completely routed. As evidence of their great demoralization, the enemy passed through Sanderson, ten miles below the battlefield, in utter disorder, every man taking care of himself, and did not halt until they reached Saint Mary's, eighteen miles below Olustee. In this battle as in the skirmishes on James Island, we met negro troops. The casualties in the regiment at Ocean Pond, were seven (7) killed and fifty-five (55) wounded. The loss in the brigade was very slight, while that of the enemy could not have been less than twenty-five hundred.

This battle by a single blow, ended the campaign in Florida, and saved the State. General Colquitt directed all moves upon the field. On the 18th of April the regiment left Florida, and on the 24th, arrived at James Island, South Carolina. On the 8th of May left Charleston, and arrived at Petersburg, Virginia, on the 11th. On the 16th of May, the regiment under the command of Lieutenant Colonel Arnold, fought most gallantly at the battle of Drewry's Bluff, Colonel Loftin being in command of a portion of Colquitt's Brigade, composed of the Sixth, Nineteenth, and Twenty-third Georgia Regiments, the Twenty-seventh and Twenty-eighth Regiments not having arrived from Petersburg. General Beauregard with about eighteen thousand men attacked and defeated General Butler, who, as the correspondents from his army stated, had forty thousand men and was besides strongly fortified. General Colquitt, though I believe the junior Brigadier present, commanded a reserve force of his own and another brigade. Early in the day the Sixth Georgia, with the other regiments of the brigade, was ordered to the extreme left to support General Ransom, who had partially succeeded in turning the enemy's right flank. The brigade at once moved over the works, and for a mile drove back the enemy, forcing him at every point of that distance to abandon his entrenchments. Our victory at Drewry's Bluff was complete; but from some cause, as has usually been the case in this war, we failed to reap the fruits. The regiment lost in this battle, twelve killed and eighty-two wounded.

On the 31st of May we reached Cold Harbor on the north side of the James River, and took position within a few hundred yards of the very spot upon which the regiment had fought on the 27th of June, 1862. On the 1st and 3d of June the enemy charged our works. On the 1st they did not come nearer than three or four hundred yards, but on the 3d their effort was a more serious one. On this day the regiment that charged in front of the Sixth Georgia, lost, as we were subsequently informed under flag of truce, by one of their own officers, eight hundred and sixty (860) men.

Our men were perfectly cool and deliberate, and almost every shot brought down its man. The ground in front of our works for a hundred yards, was literally covered with the dead and wounded. On the 3d of June the regiment left Cold Harbor, and on the 15th reached Petersburg. On the 16th the enemy made a feeble effort to charge our line, but a few well directed volleys broke their ranks. From the 15th of June up to the present, August 14th, with short intervals of rest, the regiment has been in the trenches under fire, and during that time has lost twenty-four killed and eighty wounded. Day by day, two, three, and even greater numbers would be killed or wounded. Some of our best military men think, above everything else, that this campaign in the trenches has tested the courage, endurance and patriotism of our soldiers.

On the 7th of July Lieutenant Colonel Arnold was killed in the trenches by a mortar shell from the enemy. Of all the noble and brave men who have given their lives to their country in this gigantic struggle for liberty, no braver or nobler man has fallen than Lieutenant Colonel Arnold. Gallant and fearless to a fault, these were the least of his virtues. He was the very soul of all that was honorable and true, and in a word, possessed in the highest degree, all the attributes that mark those few noble men who are an honor to their race, and who enrich the earth by their presence.

After Lieutenant Colonel Arnold was promoted to the Lieutenant Colonelcy of the regiment, the office of Major was vacant. Captain Harris has been, since his death, promoted to the Lieutenant Colonelcy, and Captain Culpepper has been promoted to the rank of Major.

The Sixth Georgia Regiment has at no time failed to charge the enemy when ordered; nor has it in a single instance fled in the face of the foe. It has had no minstrel to sing its praises, and chooses to stand alone upon its merits. It has been complimented in the highest terms by Generals D. H. Hill and Beauregard, the Generals under whom with one exception, it has fought all its battles. General Hill, who rarely compliments any one, endorsed upon an application for furlough from this regiment, these words: "Approved, because the Sixth Georgia Regiment has asked but few favors, and has acted nobly upon every battle field." General Beauregard made a similar endorsement upon a similar application. From the organization of the regiment up to the present time, the Sixth Georgia has lost two hundred and thirty-eight killed, and six hundred and thirty-nine wounded. Whatever may be the future history of the regiment, its past at least is secure.

Since the above was written, the Sixth Georgia has been again engaged on the – instant, at David's Farm, on or near the Weldon railroad. The regiment carried into action two hundred and fifty guns, and lost one killed, and thirty-one wounded and prisoners. It captured one thousand prisoners, four stand of colors, one Brigadier General and Staff, with many stands of small arms.

In February, John F. Cousins was appointed Ensign, with rank of First Lieutenant, on account of distinguished gallantry.

GEORGIA VOLUNTEERS

The record of this regiment is furnished me up to the second day of August, 1864. Owing to the absence of the regimental books, Colonel Neal has been unable to furnish me with correct statistical matter. I can, however, thanks to a report the gallant Colonel sent me from camp, written in Florida, make a correct report of the casualties occurring in battle. Owing to the incessant changes in position, and long marches of the Nineteenth, it has, no doubt, like many other Georgia regiments, lost its regimental book. I make this statement, however, upon my own authority, and may be mistaken. I will here make the statement found in the preface, that this report was written in the trenches around Petersburg, amid an incessant cannonade, with no facilities whatever for writing.

The following are the statistics of the regiment, allowing five wounded for each one killed, since the battle of Ocean Pond:

Strength of regiment since organization, ...   1,258
Killed in action, ...   184
Wounded, ...   630
Died, up to March 26th, 1864, ...   244
    Showing a real loss of, ...   607
    Showing number of deaths to be, ...   437

This loss would of course be augmented, if I could obtain the number of deaths in the regiment, since March 26th.

The above statement is not of course strictly correct; but I will again say, that, that part of it which is incorrect, is made upon the authority of no one but myself.

On the 11th day of June, 1861, the Nineteenth Regiment of Georgia Volunteers, was mustered into the service of the State of Georgia, as the Second Regiment, Fourth Brigade, of Georgia State

Troops, with the following field officers: W. W. Boyd, Colonel; Thomas C. Johnson, Lieutenant Colonel; and A. J. Hutchins, Major.

The regiment was put into camp of instruction, at Camp McDonald, and remained there until the 2d day of August, 1861, at which time the brigade was disbanded, and the regiment transferred to the Confederate States, and ordered to Lynchburg, Virginia. At that time the measles made their appearance in camp, and raged so violently in the Nineteenth Georgia, as to render it, for the period of six weeks, almost totally unfit for duty.

On the 15th day of September the regiment reached Manassas Junction, and did ordinary garrison service at that place, until the 15th of December, at which time it was attached to the Brigade of Brigadier General, now Major General Hampton, and ordered to Occognon, to protect the right flank of General Johnson's army, then at Cartersville. At this place, the regiment did picket and fatigue duty, during the winter, and were in two or three skirmishes with the enemy; in one of which, near Polwick Church, considerable damage was done the enemy, and one man of Company K, wounded, which was the first wound ever received in the regiment.

On the 10th of March, 1862, the whole army abandoned its position in front of the enemy.   Hampton's Brigade retreated to Fredericksburg, a distance of forty-five miles, and was there attached to General Whiting's Division. Nothing occurred at this place, until the 10th of April, when the forces about Fredericksburg took up the line of march for Yorktown.

The weather was very inclement.   The streams very much swollen, and the snow and rain rapidly falling, soon brought about a scene of misery hard to delineate. Many men becoming thoroughly exhausted upon the line of march, were left at the farm houses along the road, or sent to hospitals. The army reached Milford Station on the second day, and then proceeded by railroad to Ashland. From this place, the regiment again took up the line of march for Yorktown on the 15th, and after a successful and pleasant march of four days, went into encampment at Eagle Farm, near that place. General Whiting's was one of the reserve divisions at Yorktown, so that the regiment had no active duty to perform. On the 3d day of May, Yorktown was evacuated, and the retreat to Richmond began; and here also, the real hardships, privations and dangers, began. General Whiting's Division was the rear guard of the army much of the time.

While the battle of Williamsburg was being fought, the division was pushed rapidly forward to West Point, to prevent the enemy, who was landing there, from cutting off the retreat of the army. This regiment particularly, together with the balance of Hampton's Brigade, engaged the enemy near West Point, about the 12th of May, and held them in check, until the army filed past, and then, at one o'clock in the morning, resumed the retreat, under cover of the darkness, to Richmond. Hampton's Brigade was in the rear, and was frequently formed in line of battle, to repel the threatened attacks of the enemy, who closely pursued us. The weather was intensely cold, and the roads as rough and muddy as possible. Rations were very short, and indeed, every discomfort the vocabulary could name for a retreating army prevailed.

The retreat from Yorktown is still referred to in the regiment, as the greatest hardships this army has ever experienced. Nearing the Chickahominy, Whiting's Division was again hurried to the front, and halted for four days, while the whole army filed past, and then fell in the rear, and crossed the river last of all, at three o'clock, on a dark, rainy, stormy morning, after standing in the road all night. Three days after the regiment went into camp, near Richmond.

The regiment lost a large number of men from disease, contracted on the retreat from Yorktown. Many recruits had just come in, and were, of course, subject to all camp diseases. Others, old members of the regiment, were suffering from the effects of measles, and the systems of all were so affected, as to render them peculiarly liable to contract disease, from the malaria arising from the Chickahominy swamp, where we were encamped for the ensuing six weeks. Men died rapidly, and nearly all were much debilitated by the "soldier's scourge," camp diarrhea.

On the last day of May the regiment participated in the battle of Seven Pines, engaging the extreme right of the enemy; but after three unsuccessful charges, the division fell back at nine o'clock at night. The losses in this regiment in this battle, was about forty men killed and wounded. After this battle, the Nineteenth Georgia was transferred into Archer's Brigade, A. P. Hill's Light Division, and performed the usual picket and fatigue duties, in the Chickahominy swamp, until the 26th of June, on which day it went into the battle of Mechanicsville, with about four hundred men. In this battle the regiment distinguished itself, and was highly complimented by General Archer, whose character, as a stern, exacting, brave officer, rendered his compliments expressive of something. The regiment lost in this battle, one hundred and eighty-five men. The next day it was engaged in the battle of Gaines' Mill, and did its whole duty.

Loss not remembered, but it was heavy. The regiment was again engaged at Frazier's Farm, and also at Malvern Hill, with considerable loss, and was ordered to inscribe the names of the four battles upon its banner.

At Mechanicsville, Lieutenant Colonel Johnson lost his life. He was a most gallant and efficient officer, and had been in command of the regiment almost constantly from the time it reached Virginia until his death, owing to the ill health of Colonel Boyd. Major Hutchins was promoted to be Lieutenant Colonel, and Captain Neal, of Company B, to be Major. Lieutenants Dunlop and Brownfield, Company K, gallant, noble fellows, were killed at Mechanicsville, and a large number of the best officers and men in the regiment were killed, or mortally wounded, in the four battles. Lieutenant Stovall, Company A, was mortally wounded.

The Nineteenth engaged in the pursuit of McClellan's army to Harrison's Landing, and was then recalled to Richmond, and sent by railroad to Gordonsville, with General Jackson, in whose command it had been since the beginning of the battles known as the "Seven days" battles around Richmond."

On the 9th of August we were engaged in the battle of Cedar Mountain, and in it lost one-third of the men carried into action. We then commenced the march into Maryland, participating in the battles on the Rappahannock. Three days at Manassas, and at Germantown, was the command engaged, losing at Manassas (again) one-third of the men present.

Crossing the Potomac near Leesburg, this regiment entered Frederick City and remained in camp four days, at the end of which time it marched by way of Boonsborough to Williamsport, recrossed the Potomac, captured Martinsburg, and on the 13th day of September camped before Harper's Ferry. On the 15th of same month, the place was surrendered with over eleven thousand prisoners, and a vast quantity of stores of all kinds. On the morning of the 17th, the light division began the march to Sharpsburg. At two o'clock in the evening crossed the Potomac and formed into line on the extreme right, where the enemy were fast pressing back our lines. Archer's Brigade was first in line, and immediately charged the enemy without waiting for the balance of the division. The enemy in large force was driven in confusion from a strong position behind a stone fence, and the effort to turn our right flank effectually checked. In this charge more than one-half of the Nineteenth Georgia were killed and wounded. The division held its position until the night of the 18th, when it withdrew, with the army, across the Potomac. On the

20th, a force of the enemy having crossed in pursuit, Archer's Brigade and other troops turned and attacked him at Shepherdstown, inflicting serious loss on the enemy. in this affair the loss of the regiment was thirty men killed and wounded.

The regiment remained about "Bunker Hill and Berryville" until November 26th, without any event requiring notice, except a skirmish with the enemy at "Snicker's Ferry," in which forty Yankees killed and wounded, without any loss whatever to this regiment. No other infantry was engaged in this skirmish. While in the Valley much time was spent in destroying the Baltimore and Ohio railroad; also the Winchester road.

On the 26th of November the division began the march to Fredericksburg, and reached that place after an exceedingly pleasant march of twelve (12) days. On the 13th of December, 1862, the brigade occupied the right of the line, there being an interval of three hundred (300) yards between it and the next brigade on our left. The Nineteenth Georgia was situated upon the extreme left of the brigade, next to the open space between it and the next brigade. The enemy charged our front in heavier force than has ever been seen by any member of this regiment, on any field of battle in this revolution. Notwithstanding the overwhelming odds opposed to us, the assault was repulsed with most terrible loss to the enemy and comparatively small loss in this regiment. We were congratulating ourselves upon the handsome repulse we had given the enemy, when suddenly it was discovered that a large force of the enemy had passed the interval between the Nineteenth Georgia and the next brigade; and at the same time they opened fire upon our flank and rear simultaneously; some confusion occurred, as the firing became so heavy that no command could be heard. The regiment lost in this action eighty-seven (87) men, killed and wounded, and one hundred and seven (107) taken prisoners by the enemy. This is the only occasion upon which the line of this regiment has been broken, and in this case no impression was made by the attack in front.[*]

Colonel Boyd having resigned on the 12th of January, 1863, Lieutenant Colonel Hutchins was promoted Colonel, Major Neal was appointed Lieutenant Colonel, and Captain Hooper raised to the rank of Major. General Archer's Brigade went into camps near Grace Church, and on the 22d of January, the Nineteenth Georgia Regiment was transferred to General Colquitt's Georgia Brigade,

---

[*] No blame can possibly attach to this regiment for this unfortunate affair, as the reverse must have been owing to the defective line.

composed of the Sixth, Twenty-third, Twenty-seventh and Twenty-eighth Georgia Regiments, and the Thirteenth Alabama Regiment, which was exchanged for the Nineteenth Georgia.

The winter of this part of the year 1863, was spent along the Rappahannock, below Fredericksburg, until the battle of Chancellorsville and Wilderness, on the 1st and 3d of May, 1863. This regiment participated in both of said battles, losing about forty-five (45) men killed and wounded. About the 20th of May the brigade was ordered to Kinston, North Carolina, and remained quietly there until July 3d, when it was ordered to report immediately to Richmond, to repel an expected raid of the enemy. On the 9th of July it was ordered to Charleston, South Carolina, and reached that place on the 14th instant. On the 15th, two regiments of the brigade (the Sixth and Nineteenth) went to James Island, and on the 16th instant, engaged the enemy slightly, this regiment losing two men, and killing wounding or capturing sixty negroes.

Colonel Hutchins having resigned his commission on the 20th of August, 1863, Lieutenant Colonel Neal was promoted to the Colonelcy, and Major Hooper, having previously resigned, Captain Flynt was appointed Lieutenant Colonel, and Captain Mabry was promoted Major. The regiment remained in the vicinity of Charleston until the 10th of February, 1864, doing heavy duty at Battery Wagner, Fort Sumter, and Fort Johnson, and then started for Florida, but was halted and marched to Johns Island to meet a demonstration being made by the enemy; but they knowing the force which would be opposed to them, retired, and the trip to Florida was resumed; and on the 17th of February the regiment and brigade reached Olustee, Florida. On the 20th of said month the battle of Ocean Pond was fought, in which Colquitt's brigade was heavily engaged. The Nineteenth Georgia was under a heavy fire (for four hours) of small arms, and much of that time had no ammunition with which to return the fire. It had, nevertheless, captured three guns and caissons early in the battle. The loss of this regiment in this battle was ninety-seven killed and wounded. This effectual victory over the Yankees closed the campaign in Florida, and we remained quietly in camps until the 18th of April, when we were ordered to return to Virginia. The regiment made a start and had reached Florence, when we were ordered to take the back track to Sullivan's Island, Charleston harbor. It remained here but three days, when it was again ordered to Virginia, and reached Petersburg on the 13th day of May, 1864.

On the 16th of May an attack was made upon the enemy near Drewry's Bluff. The Nineteenth was engaged and lost thirty-four (34) men. It remained on the line near Bermuda Hundreds for a fortnight, and then marched to Cold Harbor, reaching that place just in time to check the advance of the enemy, who were driving our cavalry before them. Breastworks were hastily constructed at night, and at dawn the enemy charged the line, and were handsomely repulsed with sickening slaughter. The loss to the Nineteenth was trifling. This line was held under a concentrated fire of artillery for two weeks, and we left it only when the enemy abandoned his line and marched to the south side of the James River.

At Cold Harbor, the line of Colquitt's Brigade was about identical with that from which it had driven the enemy, two years before. Leaving Cold Harbor about the 15th of June, the brigade reached Petersburg at eleven o'clock, on the evening of the 16th. The enemy having taken our line of works from the local troops, at six o'clock on the same evening, we found every thing in great confusion. No information could be obtained, as to the force or position of the enemy. No one knew how much of our line they occupied. Not a picket was between the enemy and Petersburg. Haygood's South Carolina Brigade, and this, (Colquitt's,) formed a line, and began to entrench. By morning a large number of troops had arrived and were now in position to receive the expected assault.

The Yankees attacked several positions on our line, but did not molest this brigade. It having been discovered that our line was defective, on the night of the 17th the troops were all withdrawn to a line we had constructed about half a mile in the rear of our brigade. At dawn on the 18th, the enemy discovered that we were gone, and evidently thought that Petersburg was evacuated, and their way open to that city. They came charging and shouting as if no resistance was anticipated. As soon as they emerged from the woods, we unexpectedly opened fire on them, and soon effectually checked their advance. They fell back in great confusion to the woods. At two o'clock the same day, they charged the Nineteenth in very heavy force, but with the aid of the other regiments of the brigade, we succeeded in repulsing them. They left a large number of dead and wounded on the field; and indeed, so severely punished were they, that they had not since attempted an assault upon that part of the line, but have contented themselves with sharp-shooting and artillery firing upon us.

From that time until the present, the Nineteenth has been upon the same line, with occasional short intervals of rest. It has been subjected to a heavy fire of sharp-shooters and very severe shelling, especially from mortar. The duty is very heavy and has caused much sickness in the regiment.

During the fifty-two days spent here, the privations and hardships endured, have been greater than for any six months of the war. The heat in the ditches has been intense. Rations have been short. Many of the officers and men have been for six weeks without a change of clothing. yet in spite of all, they are confident and in the very best spirits. This regiment has participated in as many engagements as any other Georgia regiment, except perhaps one or two, and on no occasion has it failed to do its whole duty. It is impossible to mention individual instances of gallantry without doing injustice to many good men. The limit allowed will not admit of a more detailed account of the operations of this regiment. The Nineteenth Georgia has fought in every battle in which the Army of Northern Virginia has been engaged, except Gettysburg, Wilderness, and Spottsylvania; and in place of these, participated in the battles of Ocean Pond, Drewry's Bluff, and in the siege of Charleston, including Fort Sumter and Battery Wagner. The history of A. P. Hill's Division in the campaign of 1862, is a history of this regiment; since that time it has been identified with Colquitt's Brigade.

Independent of the above report I give names of two heroes of Georgia:–

W. J. Y. Wood, Ensign Nineteenth Georgia. From enquiry among his comrades, I find this young man is particularly noted among his comrades for an indomitable courage, which has shown conspicuous upon every battlefield, upon which his regiment has been engaged. He has repeatedly LED his regiment into action, proudly flaunting the Southern Cross in the face of the foe.

John Merritt, Company H, Nineteenth Georgia, was wounded at Ocean Pond, Florida. He obtained a furlough to return to his home in Paulding County. The retrograde movement of General Johnson's Army, left him in the Yankee lines. He was taken prisoner and sent to Todd's Barracks, Ohio. There being a number of Yankee drafted men confined with him, who were continually deserting, he conceived the bold project of escaping by representing himself as one of the deserters. He did so successfully, and after many vicissitudes, was sent to Grant's Army, where after staying several days, he managed to escape into our lines in front of Petersburg, bringing with him three Yankee deserters. General Hoke appointed him his courier immediately upon his arrival.

GEORGIA VOLUNTEERS

STATISTICAL RECORD OF TWENTY-THIRD GEORGIA VOLUNTEERS.

Number of men originally enlisted, ...	794
Number of recruits received, ...	264
Number of conscripts received, ...	37
Number of men received by transfer, ...	23
Number of officers received by appointment,	
election, promotion, and transfer, ...	13
Total strength of regiment, ...	1131

LOSSES IN OFFICERS.

Resigned for disability, ...	24
Resigned for wounds, ...	4
Resigned for other causes, ...	6
Dismissed, ...	3
Transferred, ...	7
Promoted to other commands, ...	7
Killed in action, ...	8
Died of wounds, ...	3
Died of disease, ...	2
Deserted, ...	1
Total loss in officers, ...	65

LOSSES IN ENLISTED MEN.

Discharged for disability, ...	109
Discharged by order, ...	12
Discharged by civil authority, ...	1
Discharged for promotion, ...	8
Killed in action, ...	103
Died of wounds, ...	42
Died of disease, ...	173
Transferred, ...	19
Missing in action and supposed dead, ...	6
Deserted, ...	90
Wounded in action, ...	340
Disabled by service, ...	22
* Actual loss of the regiment, ...	650
Total both permanently and	
temporarily lost, ...	990
Total loss by death, ...	337

Owing to some error, perhaps in my own calculations of statistics of this regiment, I am unable to make a correct balance. There is a difference, however, of only three men, between the report handed me and my own calculation.

It will be seen by the foregoing that the Twenty-third Georgia has lost by death three hundred and thirty-seven men; by death, discharge, promotions, transfers, &c., &c., six hundred and fifty. And counting the number of men who have been wounded, (all of whom are in all probability with the regiment now) the loss which of course is partially temporary, amounts to nine hundred and ninety men.

The Twenty-third Georgia was organized at Camp McDonald, Georgia, on the 31st day of August, 1861, entirely composed of companies from the Cherokee counties of Georgia, and were enlisted and mustered into the service for the war. The following are the names of the officers commanding the companies, and the counties to which they belong:–

---

* Independent of those wounded in action amounting to 340 men.

Company A, Captain ___ Pool, Bartow County.
Company B, Captain James H. Huggins, Union County.
Company C, Captain M. R. Ballenger, Floyd County.
Company D, Captain John Steel, Pickens County.
Company E, Captain Samuel Tate, Pickens County.
Company F, Captain B. F. King, Cobb County.
Company G, Captain J. A. Sharp, Cherokee County.
Company H, Captain F. M. Young, Walker County.
Company I, Captain Thomas Hutcherson, Gordon
    and Cherokee Counties.
Company K, Captain W. P. Barclay, Union County.

After the afore-mentioned companies were mustered into service, the organization was perfected by the election of Captain Thomas Hutcherson to the Colonelcy, Captain W. P. Barclay to the Lieutenant Colonelcy, and E. F. Best to the Majority. Dr. S. W. Thompson received the appointment of Surgeon, Dr. J. H. Spear that of Assistant Surgeon. Dr. William Bacon was appointed Assistant Quartermaster, Warren Moss, Commissary, and C. C. Sanders, Adjutant.

The regiment remained in Camp of Instruction until about the 10th day of November, 1861, when it was ordered to Richmond Virginia. Remaining at Richmond but a very short time, it was ordered to Yorktown, where it remained until the evacuation of that place, which event occurred on the 3d day of May, 1862. During this eventful siege the regiment was commanded by Lieutenant Colonel Barclay. While at this point it was assigned to the brigade of General Rains, in the division of Major General D. H. Hill.

After the retreat commenced, the regiment was on the field of the Battle of Williamsburg, but were not in the engagement. The hardships, privations and sufferings endured during this tedious retreat, were very severe, and in the opinion of many, only excelled by the disastrous retreat of Napoleon Bonaparte from Moscow. Certain it is, that no march or retreat during this war, can bear any comparison to it. The Twenty-third suffered very severely, – many men died from the sufferings and exposure they underwent; and when we reached Richmond or its vicinity, not more than one half the men and officers reported for duty.

The Battle of Seven Pines, fought upon the 31st day of May, 1862, was the first engagement in which this regiment was regularly engaged. The regiment went into the fight commanded by Lieutenant Colonel Barclay with four hundred men, and lost eighty men killed and wounded. After the fight was over, the regiment was publicly complimented by General D. H. Hill for the conspicuous gallantry which it had displayed during the fight. He said that it was owing to the manner in which the Twenty-third Georgia had conducted itself, that the tide of battle was turned in favor of the Confederate Army on that bloody day.

The next engagement in which this regiment was a participant, was the Battle of Mechanicsville, which was fought on the 26th day of June, 1862. In this fight the command of the Twenty-third Georgia devolved upon Major Best. In this action the brigade was surprised and thrown into confusion; but owing to the indefatigable exertions of Captain Huggins assisted by other officers, order was restored. Captain Huggins retained command until the enemy had disappeared from our front. The loss in the Twenty-third in this fight was slight. The regiment was engaged in the Battle of Cold Harbor the same day, and two days afterwards, participated in the Battle of White Oak Swamp, and the day afterwards, was again engaged in the terrible Battle of Malvern Hill. In all these engagements we were commanded by Captain Huggins, and lost very heavily in killed and wounded. Soon after the battles around Richmond, Lieutenant Colonel Barclay was promoted to Colonel to fill the vacancy occasioned by the resignation of Colonel Hutcherson, Major Best was promoted to Lieutenant Colonel, and Captain Huggins to Major.

The next active service performed by the regiment, was during the world-renowned campaign into the State of Maryland. The march was executed without any incident connected with the regiment worthy of notice, until the Battle of South Mountain, or as it is perhaps equally as generally called, the Battle of Boonsboro, at which place the Twenty-third Georgia acted a very conspicuous part. It held a very important position on the left of the turnpike, where it winds through a pass in the mountains, against very heavy odds, and inflicted heavy loss upon the enemy. This position was held in the face of an overpowering foe, when our ammunition was so nearly exhausted that we could only keep up a show of fight by an irregular, scattering fire. As evidence of the heat of the engagement, the loss of this gallant regiment, amounting to ninety men killed and wounded, out of three hundred carried into action, will sufficiently testify. In this fight at least seventy thousand Yankees were beaten back and kept back for many hours by Major General D. H. Hill's Division alone.

Three days after the Battle of South Mountain, the fight of Sharpsburg was inaugurated, that is, on the 17th day of September, 1862. In this dreadful fight the Twenty-third Georgia suffered very heavily. Among the number slain was the gallant Colonel Barclay, who had so often led the regiment to victory, and who had displayed conspicuous gallantry upon every field where it had been his fortune to lead. The regiment suffered an irreparable loss in his death.

After the death of Colonel Barclay, Lieutenant Colonel Best was promoted to the rank of Colonel, Major Huggins to Lieutenant Colonel, and Captain M. R. Ballenger to Major. All of these officers having been wounded, the command of the regiment devolved upon a captain for several months, during which time the regiment marched with the army from the Potomac near Shepherdstown, to Fredericksburg, the men suffering extraordinary privations upon the march, which was almost equal to the horrid retreat from Yorktown. Many of the men without a murmur, walked barefooted through the snow for days, until they were ordered by General D. H. Hill to make and wear raw hide moccasins, to which however they were very much opposed, as they were exceedingly uncomfortable.

Commanded by Captain Sharp, the regiment was in the Battle of Fredericksburg, but was not closely engaged. The loss in this fight amounted to only five killed and wounded. Shortly after this Colonel Best returned to the regiment, and was in command at the Battle of Chancellorsville, which was fought May 2d and 3d, 1863. The Twenty-third Georgia was detached from the brigade to protect a wagon train, while the army was making a flank movement. The enemy discovering our movement, and thinking that it was a retreat of the entire army, ordered General Sickles to make a reconnoissance in force, to discover what our movement really was. He obeyed the order, and at the head of twenty thousand men, marched down upon the devoted Twenty-third. He maneuvered to capture the wagon train, but after considerable skirmishing, pending which the wagon train escaped, he only succeeded in capturing one hundred and ninety men and officers of this regiment. By thus standing our ground firmly against the outrageously overwhelming numbers of the enemy, we saved the wagon train at the expense of the before enumerated prisoners. These same were exchanged about three weeks afterward and returned to the regiment.

The regiment shortly after this affair, on or about the 20th of May, was ordered to Kinston, North Carolina. After staying at Kinston a few weeks, we were ordered back to Richmond to repel a raid of the enemy's cavalry. Spending a few days at Richmond, the regiment was ordered to Wilmington, North Carolina, where after staying a few weeks, it was ordered to Charleston, South Carolina. Here it spent the winter of 1863, seeing during the time, a tour of eight days in Battery Wagner, which was certainly the most disagreeable duty the members of the Twenty-third had ever before performed. Some of our best men were lost upon this Island, number not remembered. Upon being relieved, we were placed on board the ill-fated steamer Sumter, which, as we went up the harbor, was fired upon and sunk by our guns at Fort Moultrie; but very fortunately and almost miraculously, we lost no men at all by the accident. The regiment was at this time commanded by Major Ballenger.

After the evacuation of Morris Island, fifty men of the Twenty-third were detailed for duty in Fort Sumter, where the duties were very onerous upon both officers and men. When the enemy landed upon John's Island, the Twenty-third was sent to the relief of General Wise, who was gradually retiring before them; but before the brigade to which this regiment belonged, General A. H. Colquitt's, got into position, they retired without giving battle. Immediately after this little affair, the regiment with the brigade composed of the Sixth, Nineteenth, Twenty-third, Twenty-seventh and Twenty-eighth Georgia Regiments, was ordered to report to General Finnegan, who commanded the Floridians, at Olustee in the State of Florida.

On the 20th day of February, 1864, we met the enemy at Ocean Pond, and we can truly say "veni, vidi, vici." The battle was long and bloody; but the dash and enthusiasm of our Southern boys could not be resisted. The Yankees fell into confusion, broke and fled, throwing away guns, knapsacks, accoutrements, and everything which could impede a precipitate retreat. This was one of the most signal victories that the God of war has ever allowed to perch upon our banners. The Twenty-third Georgia was commanded by Lieutenant Colonel Huggins in this fight, and acquitted itself with honor. Loss in this fight was seventy-five men out of three hundred. Very soon after the Battle of Ocean Pond, the regiment, and in fact the whole brigade, was ordered back to Charleston, South Carolina. After remaining but a very few days in Charleston, we were ordered to return to Virginia. The regiment reached Petersburg while the enemy held the Richmond and Petersburg railroad.

We made a very hard march in one night from Petersburg to Drewry's Bluff, around the flank of the enemy, with the remainder of the brigade, as an escort to General Beauregard. The regiment was in the Battle of Drewry's Bluff on the 16th of May, commanded by Major Ballenger. The Twenty-third, advanced with two other regiments of the brigade, half a mile in front of the main line of our army, and drove the enemy from a thick piece of woods where they had taken position. We afterwards crossed the road with the other regiments, in the rear of the enemy, and drove them from their breastworks, which they held in front of our men. The victory over the Federals at this point was complete; but its results were not as great as might have been suspected, for the great advantage we had gained over them was not followed up as it might have been, owing perhaps, or I should say no doubt, to some cause which has not been made public, or which was not known to the army itself.

The next move of the regiment was to Cold Harbor, where on the 1st and 3d days of June it nobly repulsed the desperate charges of the enemy, inflicting the most severe punishment on the drunken rabble of Grant. The ground was literally covered with the slain of the enemy, with a very trifling loss on our part. The regiment was here commanded by Major Ballenger. This was the second time this command had met the enemy upon the field of Cold Harbor, and the position of the Twenty-third was nearly identical with that it occupied two years before, about the 27th or 28th of June, 1862.

Grant's move to the south side of the James caused another movement of the army; and Colquitt's Brigade moved to Petersburg, where it held an important position in the line during the siege, and repulsed two assaults of the enemy upon the line. The labor and hardships were very severe here, but were well borne and endured with the greatest fortitude by the troops of a young nation struggling to be free. Colonel Huggins, who had recently been promoted to fill the vacancy occasioned by the dismissal of Colonel Best, commanded during the siege. The enlisted men have borne their part most nobly throughout the war, and deserve the highest plaudits of their countrymen.

The following are the names of persons noted for their gallantry, but for the want of proper records, the peculiar acts of bravery by which they are distinguished, cannot be given.

Captain A. Young, Company K; Captain M. R. Ballenger, Company C; Lieutenant William F. Smith, Company I; Joseph Adkins, Company B; Lieutenant J. M. Steel, Company I; Corporal J. M. Reeves, Company D; Privates R. C. Brock and John Hambrick, Company E; and Private E. D. Cullence; at Seven Pines.

Privates H. H. McGuire, H. Elison, D. H. House, in the Battles before Richmond.

J. B. Fulton, B. C. Fulton, J. A. Cosner, and L. P. Parker, Company I, at South Mountain, Maryland.

A great many other officers and men have performed equally as gallant acts as those whose names appear above; but the officers commanding have usually refused to make any distinctions where nearly all act their part well.

Owing to the frequent changes in the officers commanding this regiment, there has been no correct record kept of dates, battles, &c., and I have been compelled to supply the dates in most cases myself. Many of them may therefore be incorrect, but they are very nearly right. Below I subjoin a letter from Colonel Huggins, which will place him and his regiment right before the public, as regards the limited material with which he has supplied me.

Petersburg, Virginia, August 3d, 1864.

COLONEL FOLSOM,—*Dear Sir:—*I enclose to you a very imperfectly arranged history of the Twenty-third Georgia, prepared under circumstances that make it next to impossible to make it which it should be. No record of battles, marches and events has been kept, consequently this report is made almost entirely from memory. Besides the foregoing, we are constantly on the front lines, near the enemy, and have but little time to devote to such duties, notwithstanding we fell deeply interested in your history of the regiments from our noble old mother State.

With high regard and esteem,
Your obedient servant,
JAMES H. HUGGINS,
Colonel commanding Twenty-third Georgia Regiment.

TWENTY-EIGHTH REGIMENT

GEORGIA VOLUNTEERS

———

The Twenty-eighth Regiment of Georgia Volunteers, then known as the Twentieth Regiment, was organized at Camp Stephens near Griffin, Georgia, on the 4th day of September, 1861, by the election of T. J. Worthen from Washington County, as Colonel; G. A. Hall from Merriwether, as Lieutenant Colonel, and James G. Cain from Jefferson, as Major. On the 10th of September the regiment was mustered into the Confederate service by Major Calhoun, and was then composed of the following eight companies, two having been previously ordered by Governor Brown to different commands:–Companies A, B and H, from Washington County; Company C from Richmond; Company D from Cherokee; Company E from Merriwether; Company I from Jefferson, and Company K from Emanuel.

The regiment remained at Camp Stephens for instruction in the drill and manual, until the 4th of November. On the 25th of September the ladies of Merriwether County presented to the regiment a most beautiful Confederate banner, which was received by Captain Crawford of Company C, with a few happy and eloquent remarks. On the 4th of November the regiment received orders to proceed to Richmond, where it arrived on the 8th, and encamped on Fulton Hill near the city. While here two companies which had formerly been attached to the Eighteenth Georgia Regiment, Company F from Cherokee, and Company G from Gordon Counties, were attached to this regiment, thus completing the required number of companies for its proper organization. At the same time the regiment was known at the War Department as the Twenty-eighth Regiment of Georgia Volunteers, several Georgia regiments having been previously mustered into the Confederate service, independent of the state organization.

On the 17th of November the regiment received orders to proceed to Manassas Junction, and arrived at that place on the 18th.

Here it remained on post duty until the 30th of December, when it moved into winter quarters about one mile and a half from the Junction. During this time the regiment suffered severely from disease, and a great many valuable men were lost. Diseases were more frequent and dangerous, as many of the men had but just recovered from attacks of measles and camp fever, contracted during their stay in Georgia, relapsed again on account of the cold climate and the cold and inclement weather, during which they were greatly exposed by night standing guard, and by day doing fatigue duty. And their diseases would frequently end in their death, as our hospital accommodations were very limited, and in some cases even the sick were not properly cared for with the necessary attentions. During one period, the diseases in the regiment were so frequent and severe, that the *aggregate* number reported for duty did not amount to more than forty (40) men. Toward the beginning of February, 1862, the regiment recovered in a considerable degree its health.

Upon the 18th of February the Twenty-eighth Georgia received orders to leave Manassas Junction, and upon that memorable retreat it only had a very few sick. At Manassas the regiment was armed with the Springfield musket, having come from Georgia unarmed. On the 19th of February the regiment took up the line of march southward, having previously been joined to a brigade with the Twenty-seventh Georgia, Fourth North Carolina, and Forty-ninth Virginia Regiments, under command of Colonel G. W. Anderson, of North Carolina. After two days of marching the regiment arrived at the Rappahannock river, and after fording that stream near Rappahannock Station on the Orange and Alexandria railroad, encamped near the southern bank. Here the troops remained about a week, when they again, in conjunction with the brigade, took up the line of march, and passing through Culpepper Court House, crossed the Rapidan river near Rapidan Station on the Orange and Alexandria railroad, and encamped upon Clark's Mountain, about four miles from the river. Here the regiment remained until about the 4th of April, 1862, when it proceeded by railroad to Richmond, and from thence on a steamboat down the James river to King's Landing, about fifteen miles from Yorktown, at which place the regiment, after a hot and tedious march, arrived on the evening of the 5th of April, 1862.

One day after its arrival at Yorktown, the regiment under the command of Lieutenant Colonel Hall, Colonel Worthen being sick, was assigned a position outside of the works surrounding the town, in a ravine, and during the stay there performed picket and out-post duty along the banks of the river. After two weeks the regiment was moved inside of the works, but on a high hill, exposed to the shell from the enemy's gunboats, which annoyed us very frequently.

On the 2d of May, 1862, we had the misfortune to lose Lieutenant Colonel Hall, who died of typhoid pneumonia when he was about to be conveyed on board of a vessel for his removal to Richmond. Colonel Hall's loss was severely felt by this regiment. A gentleman of great talents and high mind, he had won the love and esteem of his officers and men, and although not actually engaged in battle, had shown that bravery and coolness in moments of expected danger, especially while performing out-post duty at Yorktown, which eminently fitted him for the position he occupied.

While at Yorktown we lost Captain Hill of Company G, severely wounded in the arm, and two men. On the night of the 2d the regiment left its position at Yorktown, in pursuance of orders, but was soon recalled, and reoccupied its position until the night of the 3d, when Yorktown was evacuated, and it marched to Williamsburg, a distance of fifteen miles, where it arrived on the morning of the 4th. Here the men rested until the morning of the 5th, when they again resumed the line of march; but they had hardly proceeded two miles, when the brigade was ordered to return at the double-quick to Williamsburg, where a battle was raging between ours and the Yankee forces. The men threw away their blankets, knapsacks, overcoats, and everything which impeded their hasty march to the battle field; but when they arrived there, although eager for the fray, the regiment was held in reserve, and was only destined to be inactively exposed to the fire of the enemy.

The regiment remained upon the field of battle that night, the 5th, and the sufferings of that night will long be remembered. A cold, drizzling rain had been falling all day, and continued during the night. The men stood knee deep in mud, and had nothing to shelter them from the rain, or shield them from the cold, having, as has been previously mentioned, thrown away their overcoats and blankets on the double-quick march. The sufferings were the more severe, as most of the men had had no provisions to appease their hunger for the past twenty-four hours, and the commissary wagons were about ten miles in advance of the army.

On the 6th the army again marched towards *Burnt Ordnance*, but still without their hunger having been appeased, where they arrived the same night. Here the regiment received a very small supply of provisions, hardly sufficient for supper; and although the different commissaries tried their utmost, they were not able to supply the men with rations until after the regiment had again resumed the line of march, and proceeded a few miles on the morning of the 7th. As soon as General Featherstone, who had been assigned to the command of our brigade, (General D. H. Hill's Division) received information that the commissaries had received supplies of provisions, he halted the brigade, and ordered the provisions to be divided and cooked, and the men were allowed to refresh themselves by rest until afternoon, when the road was again filled by our marching column. After a great deal of suffering, and marching through mud ankle and knee deep, and but very scantily fed, the troops arrived at Long Bridge on the Chickahominy River, about the 10th instant.

At this place the regiment remained and rested until the 20th. Supplies were still very scarce, and sometimes the men had to content themselves with one cracker and a very small piece of bacon per day.

On the 20th the troops were again put in motion, and arrived the same evening within three miles of Richmond. Here ended the memorable retreat from Yorktown, during which the sufferings, occasioned by the disagreeable weather, muddy and miry roads, hard marching and starving, had never been surpassed since the beginning of the war. Arriving at the Capitol, the troops were permitted to rest, and as supplies became more plentiful and regular, the men were enabled to recuperate rapidly. While here, Major J. G. Cain was promoted to the Lieutenant Colonelcy, vice Lieutenant Colonel Hall, deceased, and Captain Tully Graybill, of Company A, promoted to Major.

On the morning of the 30th of May, the wagons belonging to the brigade were ordered within the works around Richmond, and preparations made within betokened a coming engagement. On the morning of the 31st, the Twenty-eighth Georgia marched to the battle ground of Seven Pines. The battle did not commence until about two o'clock, P.M., when D. H. Hill's Division, occupying the right wing, made the attack, driving the enemy before it. The Twenty-eighth was commanded, in this engagement, by Captain John N. Wilcox, of Company K, the senior officer present–Colonel Worthen being severely ill in Richmond, and Lieutenant Colonel Cain and Major Graybill absent for other sufficient reasons. Captain Wilcox commanded the regiment ably and with great skill, and that the Twenty-eighth bore a prominent and noble part in this engagement, its casualties, amounting to one hundred and thirty-four killed and wounded, sufficiently show. This loss was from only eight companies, as two of the largest companies were detailed to support a battery. The day on which this battle was fought had been extremely wet and disagreeable, a heavy rain having fallen, and the men were compelled to wade knee deep in mud and water; but this by no means cooled their ardor, but only incited them to fresher deeds of daring, which carried them on to victory. The brigade was commanded by Colonel Anderson, of the Fourth North Carolina, General Featherstone being detained by sickness. In the battle of the Seven Pines, no regiment in the brigade fought with more gallantry and bravery then the Twenty-eighth Georgia.

The next morning Major Graybill was, by accident, taken prisoner on his way to rejoin his command, he having by mistake passed our pickets and entered the Yankee lines. Lieutenant Colonel Cain again took command of the regiment, which remained in camp until the 12th of June, drilling and performing fatigue and various other duties, when it moved camp and was formed into another brigade with the Sixth, Twenty-third, and Twenty-seventh Georgia, and Thirteenth Alabama Regiments.

On the 20th, General Featherstone having been assigned to another brigade, Colonel A. H. Colquitt took command, and it has ever since been known as "Colquitt's Brigade." Here also Colonel Worthen rejoined the regiment and resumed command.

On the 26th the brigade was moved to the Mechanicsville turnpike, where the first of the series of engagements was fought, generally known as the "Battles around Richmond." Our division, under command of Major General D. H. Hill, was engaged in nearly all of these battles, and the regiment bore its proportionate share in them, losing during the different engagements sixty-five in killed and wounded. In the battle of Malvern Hill, Colonel Worthen was mortally, and Lieutenant Colonel Cain severely wounded. Colonel Worthen died at Richmond, whither he had been conveyed, on the 3d of July. The regiment has deeply mourned his loss, even as they would have mourned the loss of a father. Kind, affable and affectionate, at the same time commanding that respect due to his station, he had won the love of his men and the esteem and veneration of his officers. Although nearly sixty years of age, he entered the army for the defence of his country as captain of Company B, from which position he was elected to the Colonelcy of the regiment; and during the memorable *seven days fight* around Richmond, he led his regiment in all the engagements, although not quite recovered from a severe attack of pneumonia, and when he fell, it was in *front* of his regiment, leading it on to glory and victory.

After the battles around Richmond, the regiment encamped about three miles from the city, on the York River railroad, where it remained until the 19th day of August, 1862, when it was moved by rail to Orange Court House. In the meantime, Major Graybill, who had been exchanged, returned and took command of the regiment. From Orange Court House the regiment proceeded, on the 26th of August, to the Rapidan river, and, after crossing it, proceeded, through Culpepper Court House, Warrenton and Gainsville, to the battle field of Manassas number two, but did not reach there in time to participate in that glorious victory. From Manassas the regiment moved, by Chantilly and Drainesville, to Leesburg, where we arrived on the 4th of September. On the 5th the regiment again took up the line of march, and, passing through Leesburg to the Point of Rocks, crossed the Potomac river on the night of the 5th of September. The next morning the regiment proceeded by Buckeyetown, Maryland, to within four miles of Frederick City. Here the regiment pitched camp and remained until the 12th, when it again moved, through Frederick City, by Middletown, to Boonsboro, where it arrived that evening. This same evening Colquitt's Brigade was ordered back to South Mountain, a spur of the Blue Ridge, on the turnpike between Frederick City and Boonsboro. On the morning of the 14th the enemy made his appearance and immediately engaged Garland's Brigade. General D. H. Hill having, by that time, moved up the whole of his division, the engagement became general. The Twenty-eighth, in conjunction with the Twenty-third Georgia Regiment, held a position on the turnpike, protected by a stone fence, and although the enemy, in overwhelming numbers, repeatedly charged their position, these two regiments as repeatedly drove them back with heavy loss, and maintained their position until they were recalled late at night by order of Gen. Colquitt. The regiment on this occasion was commanded by Major Graybill, who displayed perfectly the talents of a commander. He very narrowly escaped being wounded, as his coat and vest were perforated in several places by Yankee bullets. The casualties amounted to forty (40) in killed, wounded and missing.

On the night of the 14th the regiment again moved by way of Sharpsburg, Maryland, to the banks of the Potomac opposite Shepherdstown, Virginia, where it arrived on the morning of the 15th. On the morning of the 16th the division occupied the centre of the line of battle near Sharpsburg, and on the morning of the 17th the regiment participated in that sanguinary conflict, which lasted until late at night. Here we lost seventy (70) men in killed and wounded; among the latter, Captain Garrison, of Company D, a gallant and efficient officer, who acted as Major during the fight. In this place, also, mention should be made of Lieutenant J. W. Banning, of Company E, who, during the engagement, had to take command of the regiment because of the loss of superior commanders, and who, by his skill and bravery, won the admiration of his men and the praise of his superior officers.

On the 18th the regiment remained in line of battle on the ensanguined field, and at night recrossed the Potomac at Shepherdstown, and retreated towards Martinsburg, where the army arrived on the 22d, remained until the 28th, and arrived at Bunker Hill, twelve miles from Winchester, Virginia, on the night of the 30th of September, 1862. The regiment left that place on the 18th of October, and proceeded to Charlestown, where it participated in destroying the Winchester and Harper's Ferry railroad; left Charlestown on the morning of the 20th, and after crossing the Shenandoah River at Berry's Ferry on the 23d, encamped between Paris and Upperville. On the morning of the 25th of October the army was drawn up in line of battle between those two places, expecting the enemy to attack; but on the morning of the 26th the army again marched up the Shenandoah river to Front royal, where it arrived that evening. On the 27th the army again laid in line of battle, and on the night of the 28th it crossed the south fork of the Shenandoah river, and went into camps about three miles from Front Royal. On the 30th of October the regiment marched for Strasburg, Virginia, where it arrived that evening remained there until the 20th of November, when it again moved by Woodstock and New Market, across the Massenothan range, and crossed the Blue Ridge on the 23d, and camped that night near a little village called Craiglesville. On the 24th the regiment proceeded by Madison Court House, and encamped within two miles of Gordonsville. Here it remained until the 27th, when it again moved by Orange Court House to Fredericksburg, near which place it encamped on the night of the 29th. Next day it moved to Guinea's Station, and from thence, on the 1st of December, to Port Royal, near the Rappahannock river, where it remained until the morning of the 12th, and then moved to Hamilton's Crossing, and on the morning of the 13th to the battle field of Fredericksburg. In this battle the Division of General D. H. Hill was not actively engaged, but was exposed to the fire of the enemy, and the regiment lost ten men in killed and wounded.

On the 15th the regiment moved into camps about three miles from Guinea's Station, and went into winter quarters;

nevertheless, the division performed picket duty on the Rappahannock river during the winter. Nothing of importance occurred until the morning of the 28th of April, 1863, when the regiment was ordered to proceed to Hamilton's Crossing, on the R. & F. and P. R. R., and formed in line of battle, expecting an attack from the enemy, who was crossing the Rappahannock river at different fords. On the night of the 20th the brigade marched to the battle ground of Chancellorsville and Wilderness, and participated in the engagements of the 1st and 2d of May, 1863, where the regiment, under command of Colonel Graybill, who had been promoted from Major after Lieutenant Colonel Cain had resigned, lost twenty-five men in killed and wounded. The regiment remained on the battle field until the evening of the 5th, a fit anniversary for the terrible night of May 5th, 1862, for it rained tremendously, and the roads were in an awful condition. On the evening of the 6th the regiment returned to their old camp near Guinea's Station. Here it remained until the 22d, when the brigade was ordered to proceed to Kinston, North Carolina, where it arrived May 24th. While here the regiment performed picket duty until the 3d day of July, 1863, when it was ordered back to Richmond to aid in repelling a raid of the enemy. On the 9th of July we were ordered to Topsail Inlet, about fifteen miles from Wilmington.

August 8th, the regiment proceeded to Charleston, South Carolina, arriving there on the 10th. On its arrival at Charleston, the regiment was ordered to James Island, where it established camps near Fort Pemberton, on the west lines. On the night of the 30th of August, the Twenty-seventh and Twenty-eighth Georgia Regiments, of this Brigade, were ordered to relieve the garrisons of Batteries Wagner and Gregg, on Morris Island. The regiments remained there until the night of the evacuation, on the 7th of September. During the stay of the Twenty-eighth on Morris Island, the regiment was subjected to the severest shelling it has ever experienced during the war, and was exposed to the most imminent danger, being obliged to keep a close watch from the ramparts of the Fort. Captain W. P. Crawford, of Company C, commanded the regiment during its stay on Morris Island, and his conduct while in command has endeared him to the whole regiment. Here, too, must be recorded the death of the brave and gallant Captain John R. Haines, of Company B, who was killed by a shell just as he had taken command of, and was in the act of leading, a detachment of one hundred picked men, of whom fifty belonged to the Twenty-eighth Georgia, to repel a threatened attack of the enemy in the rear of Battery Wagner. Colonel Keitt, commanding Battery Wagner, had requested Captain Crawford to furnish him a competent and trustworthy officer, and Captain Haines was the officer selected.

The casualties of the regiment during its occupation of Morris Island were thirty-four killed and wounded. After the evacuation of Morris Island, the regiment went into winter quarters. During the winter the regiment performed picket duty, alternately, at Secessionville and Battery Pringle, also at Fort Johnson, and made part of the garrison of Fort Sumter. During the heavy bombardment of that Fort, the regiment lost twenty men in killed and wounded.

On the 8th day of February, 1864, the regiment was ordered to John's Island, where it aided in repelling the enemy to his gunboats. From thence it proceeded to Lake City, Florida, where it arrived on the 16th of February. On the 20th of February Colquitt's Brigade proceeded to Olustee Station, about ten miles from Lake City, where it encountered a heavy force of the enemy, composed of blacks and whites. Other troops having come up, a general engagement ensued, in which Colquitt's Brigade acted the chief part, and was mainly instrumental in winning the glorious victory of Ocean Pond. The regiment here fought with undoubted bravery, driving the enemy before them; and although at one time out of ammunition, the men nobly stood their ground, and as soon as reinforcements and ammunition arrived, they charged the enemy and finally helped to drive him from the field. It is but meet to mention the conspicuous gallantry of Color-bearer Sergeant Tiffany, (which was noticed by General Colquitt,) who fell, and also the gallantry of William Patton, of Company C, who took the colors and carried them safely through the fight; and also the gallantry of Lieutenant Rowe, of Company E, while planting the colors of the regiment over two Napoleon guns captured from the enemy. The chivalric Captain Crawford, assisted by the brave Captain Banning, commanded the regiment in this engagement. Captain Crawford was severely wounded in the leg while leading his men, and had to leave the command to Captain Banning, who, although he had received a painful wound, refused to leave the field, and with the blood streaming from his wound led his men to victory. A few days after the battle, Captain Crawford was promoted to Lieutenant Colonel and Captain J. W. Banning to Major. The regiment remained at Camp Milton until the last of March, when it moved to Baldwin, when it was complimented by Major General Anderson, commanding district of Florida, for the zeal and activity which they displayed in throwing up fortifications: the compliment was issued in a General Order. April 19th, the regiment left Baldwin for Charleston, South Carolina; remained in Charleston, doing provost duty, until the 10th of May, when it proceeded to Petersburg, Virginia, to rejoin the rest of the brigade, which had preceded it a few days before.

May 16th, battle of Drury's Bluff was fought, and this regiment was temporarily attached to Martin's Brigade, which attacked the enemy, but the Twenty-eighth Georgia was not actively engaged. On the 18th of May it rejoined Colquitt's Brigade, and took position in the line in Chesterfield County. While there a charge was made on the 20th of May, in which a detachment of one hundred men from the regiment participated, under command of Captain J. A. Johnson, of Company H. The detachment succeeded in driving the enemy from his line, but with heavy loss, losing twenty in killed and wounded–among the former Captain William M. Wood, of Company A.

May 31st, the regiment proceeded to Cold Harbor, in front of Richmond, and took their position in the trenches. On the 2d of June the enemy made a heavy charge, and succeeded in breaking that portion of the line held by Clingham's North Carolina Brigade; but the Twenty-seventh Georgia, supported by the Twenty-eighth, charged in gallant style from their position, and succeeded in retaking the lost part of the line. In this brilliant little affair Major J. W. Banning was severely wounded in the hip, and a considerable number of men killed and wounded. The enemy charged repeatedly upon our lines during their siege of Richmond, but were always repulsed with heavy slaughter.

On the 13th the regiment moved to Malvern Hill, and on the 15th recrossed the James and Appomattox rivers, and arrived just in time with the Division (General Hokes') to repel an attack the enemy made on the second line of breastworks around Petersburg. Here the regiment occupied a position in the trenches which has tried the fortitude and endurance of the men to the greatest degree. The enemy, having planted a battery of mortars in front of their position, shelled the regiment with great precision, killing and wounding a considerable number. A few men were lost, though not engaged, in the battle of the 30th of July. The loss of the regiment from June 1st to this day, (August 13th) amounts to eighty-two killed and wounded.

Adjutant Thomas O. Wicker of Washington County deserves special mention in connection with the Twenty-eighth Georgia. This gallant and meritorious young officer enlisted as a private in the Washington Rifles, First Georgia Volunteer Regiment, organized March 18th, 1861. He passed through the arduous campaign in Northern Virginia under General Garnett. Upon the regiment being mustered out of service, he organized a company of artillery and was elected First Lieutenant; but upon being tendered the position of Adjutant of the Twenty-eighth Georgia, he resigned his commission and accepted the appointment. Owing to the provisions of the Promotion Act, adjutants of regiments were thrown entirely out of the line of promotion. Hence, Adjutant Wicker still holds his original position.

He has illustrated in his own person, upon many bloody battle fields of this war, the character of the Georgia troops. He has been most honorably mentioned several times in official reports for his coolness and conspicuous courage. He has now been strongly recommended by Major General Hoke and Brigadier General Colquitt, for promotion for his gallantry.

Since the foregoing was written, I have received from Adjutant T. O. Wicker the following

STATISTICAL RECORD,

Number of men killed in action, ...	153
Number of men died of disease or wounds,	243
Total deaths, ...	396

Discharged, ...	70
Resigned, ...	24
Total real loss, ...	490
Wounded in action, ...	280
Total real and temporary loss, ...	770

GEORGIA VOLUNTEERS

———

STATISTICAL RECORD.

Number of men originally enlisted, ...	684
Number of recruits and conscripts, ...	<u>467</u>
Total strength of regiment, ...	1151

LOSSES.

Number of men killed in action, ...	104
Number of men died of wounds,	
disease, &c., ...	<u>268</u>
Loss by death, ...	372
Number of men discharged, &c., ...	<u>174</u>
Total loss of regiment, ...	546

CHANGES IN FIELD OFFICERS.

The original field officers elected were:–Levi B. Smith, of Talbotton, Colonel; S. L. Brewer, of Taylor County, Lieutenant Colonel; Charles T. Zachry, of Henry County, Major.

Lieutenant Colonel Brewer resigned in December, 1861, and Major Zachry was elected Lieutenant Colonel, and Captain H. B. Halliday elected Major. Major Halliday resigned in August, 1862, and senior Captain John W. Stubbs was appointed Major. Colonel L. B. Smith was killed at Sharpsburg on the 17th of September, 1862, and Lieutenant Colonel Zachry was appointed Colonel to fill the vacancy. Major Stubbs was appointed Lieutenant Colonel, and senior Captain Charles J. Dennis was appointed Major. Major Dennis resigned in December, 1862, and Captain Jasper N. Dorsey appointed Major. Lieutenant Colonel Stubbs resigned in December, 1862, and Major Dorsey was appointed Lieutenant Colonel. First Lieutenant and Adjutant James Gardner, promoted to Major for distinguished gallantry in action. Lieutenant Colonel Dorsey was dismissed the service in May, 1864, by sentence of General Court Martial, and Major Gardner appointed Lieutenant Colonel. Captain H. Bussey appointed Major. Lieutenant Colonel Gardner was killed on the 18th of June, 1864, and Major Bussey was appointed Lieutenant Colonel.

The Twenty-seventh Regiment of Georgia Volunteer Infantry was organized at Camp Stephens, near Griffin, Georgia, and was mustered into the service of the Confederate States on the 9th and 10th days of September, 1861.

On the 31st of October it was ordered to Richmond, Virginia, and thence to Manassas, where it arrived about the 15th of November, without arms. The first service it rendered was in the building of a bridge across the Occoquan river, which was completed about the 15th of December, when the regiment was ordered into winter quarters at Camp Pickens, near Manassas. At this point the regiment performed garrison duty until the 9th day of March, 1862, when they were ordered to Clark's Mountain. Colonel G. B. Anderson, of North Carolina, was commanding the brigade, composed of the Fourth North Carolina Troops, the Forty-ninth Virginia Infantry, and the Twenty-seventh and Twenty-eighth Georgia Volunteer Regiments. The brigade arrived at Clark's Mountain on the 20th of March, 1862. On the 9th of April, Brigadier General W. S. Featherstone was assigned to and assumed command of the brigade. While encamped at Clark's Mountain the weather was very inclement, and the troops suffered exceedingly.

On the evening of the 9th of April, the regiment marched to the railroad to take the cars for Richmond, through snow and sleet from four to six inches in depth. Upon the arrival of the regiment in the city, they were ordered to take boat for Grover's Landing on the James river, (this was on the 10th of April) and from thence were marched across the country to Yorktown. On the 14th day of April the Twenty-seventh Georgia Regiment, with the Thirteenth Alabama Regiment, was ordered in front of the works to assist Captain Hardaway's Battery in dislodging some sharpshooters, who were annoying us to a considerable extent, from a pine grove between our works and those of the enemy. The orders being successfully carried out, the sharpshooters having been dislodged, the regiment returned to camp jubilant over their first engagement with the enemy, without the loss of a single life. On the evening of May 3d, the regiment commenced its retreat with the whole army from Yorktown; it passed through Williamsburg on the 4th, and on the morning of the 5th the retreat was resumed. The Twenty-seventh Georgia had marched about five miles, when orders were received for it to return to Williamsburg in *double-quick time*, to assist our troops in the battle of Williamsburg, which was then raging. The rain was falling, the roads were in a terrible condition, and the weather was extremely cold; the regiment, however, caring nothing for these discomforts, about faced, (instead of countermarching) and started at the double-quick. Arriving at Williamsburg, knapsacks, haversacks, blankets, and every thing which could interfere with their efficiency in battle were thrown off, by our boys, as quickly as possible.

A position was assigned to the Twenty-seventh Georgia beyond and to the left of the town. This position they occupied for several hours, when they were marched to another position in a large wheat field, where they remained during the night, suffering immensely from cold, fatigue, and the knawing pangs of hunger.

About two o'clock on the morning of the 6th, the wheat field was evacuated and the line of march resumed toward the city of Richmond. Upon the arrival of the regiment at Long Bridge, they struck camp and remained there for ten or twelve days, and then moved to the vicinity of Richmond.

At the battle of Seven Pines, fought on the 31st of May, this regiment participated, going into action at two o'clock in the afternoon, a little to the left of the Williamsburg road. General Featherstone being sick, the command of the brigade devolved upon Colonel G. B. Anderson, of North Carolina. Colonel Smith, of this regiment, was wounded in the early part of the engagement, but did not quit the field until the brigade was relieved. About four o'clock, P.M., Colonel Jenkins, of South Carolina, with his sharpshooters, came to the relief of the Twenty-seventh Georgia, when a charge was ordered and the enemy were completely routed in front of their position. At this juncture the brigade was relieved, excepting the Twenty-seventh Georgia, who were ordered to keep in supporting distance of Colonel Jenkins, who was then in pursuit of the enemy, and render him any assistance which might be necessary. Just before sundown Colonel Jenkins ordered Lieutenant Colonel Zachry (who was then in command of the Twenty-seventh Georgia, Colonel Smith having retired) to form on his (Colonel Jenkins') right, as the enemy in heavy force were attempting to flank him in that direction. The regiment moved up at the double-quick, and were forming line, when some little confusion occurred, which lasted, however, but a moment. It was at this time that Adjutant Gardner displayed that coolness and marked bravery which elicited from Colonel Jenkins a personal compliment and recommendation for promotion. Colonel Jenkins succeeded, with the aid of the Twenty-seventh Georgia, in baffling the designs of the enemy upon our flank, and drove him one-fourth of a mile from their position, when night put an end to the conflict. The loss of the Twenty-seventh Georgia in this engagement was severe, amounting to one hundred and fifty-four (154) killed and wounded.

After the battle of Seven Pines a brigade was formed, consisting of the Sixth, Twenty-third, Twenty-seventh and Twenty-eighth Georgia Regiments, and the Thirteenth Alabama Regiment, General Featherstone commanding. In a few days, however, General Featherstone was assigned to duty elsewhere, and the command of the brigade devolved upon Colonel A. H. Colquitt, commanding the Sixth Georgia Regiment.

On the morning of the 26th of June the regiment took up the line of march at half past one o'clock, and halted near Mechanicsville. The regiment was engaged in the battle of Mechanicsville on the morning of the 27th, and at Cold Harbor on the evening of the same day. At the battle of Cold Harbor, Gen. Colquitt's Brigade charged the enemy and gained a very important position, which was held by the Twenty-seventh for some time, without any assistance from the other regiments of the brigade. The Sixty-first Georgia Regiment was ordered forward to relieve the Twenty-seventh, but, mistaking them for the enemy, fired into the regiment, until Adjutant Gardner could pass from the extreme right of the regiment to its centre, and have the colors raised, by that means signifying to them that we were friends. The Sixty-first, recognizing the colors, ceased firing, and coming quickly forward, relieved the Twenty-seventh.

This regiment next engaged the enemy at White Oak Swamp, on the evening of the 31st of June; and again on the evening of the 1st of July, at Malvern Hill, we were hurled upon the foe, losing very severely in killed and wounded, Adjutant Gardner being among those who were severely wounded.

About the 6th of July the regiment returned to the vicinity of Richmond, having suffered a loss of one hundred and twenty-six men, killed and wounded, in the series of engagements, known as the battles around Richmond.

From the 10th of July until the 17th of August, the Twenty-seventh Georgia marched several times from the vicinity of Richmond to Malvern Hill and back, when the movements of the enemy would indicate an advance from that point.

On the 19th of August the regiment took the cars at Richmond, and proceeded to Orange Court House, where it remained until the 27th of August, when it took up the line of march, and joined Generals Lee and Jackson near Fairfax, Virginia, two days after the second battle of Manassas, where it rested twenty-four hours, and then proceeded, *via* Leesburg to Frederick, Maryland. After resting three days at Frederick, it marched *via* South Mountain and Boonsboro, to within six miles of Hagerstown, Maryland; when orders were received to return at once to South Mountain pass, which was performed on the night of the 12th of September. On the morning of the 14th, a position was assigned to the Twenty-seventh by Major General D. H. Hill, to whose division Colquitt's Brigade belonged; which position it held all that day. At night we were withdrawn and marched to Sharpsburg, from thence to the north bank of the Potomac, opposite Shepherdstown, Virginia, where we arrived about eleven o'clock on the morning of the 15th. On the morning of the 16th, the brigade was marched back to Sharpsburg, and assigned to different positions during the day. On the morning of the 17th, the Twenty-seventh Georgia Regiment went into the fight early in the morning, and fought long and well. Among the many fatal casualties in the Twenty-seventh, was Colonel Smith, as gallant and generous a heart as ever beat, and whose loss will be long deplored by his surviving comrades Lieutenant Colonel Zachry was severely wounded in this engagement.

The loss of the Twenty-seventh Georgia in the battles of South Mountain and Sharpsburg, amounted to one hundred and forty-nine (149) men killed and wounded.

Leaving Sharpsburg on the morning of the 19th, the regiment crossed the Potomac river before day, and marched to Martinsburg, where it rested two or three days, and then proceeded to Bunker Hill. We left Bunker Hill about the 23d of October, and assisted in tearing up the railroad, leading from Harper's Ferry to Charlestown, on or about the night of the 24th of September. Here again the troops suffered incredibly from the excessive cold, the men being generally poorly clad, and in many instances barefooted, their sufferings were very severe. After destroying the above mentioned railroad, the regiment marched across the Shenandoah river, and camped between Paris and Upperville, about the 1st of November.

Leaving Paris it marched to Front Royal, thence to Strasburg, where another railroad was destroyed.

Between the 15th and 20th of November, we were ordered to march, and passing Guinea's Station *via* Orange Court House, arrived at our destination in the vicinity of Port Royal, on the Rappahannock, on the 1st day of December. The troops on this march made an average of twenty-two miles per day, and large numbers of them were forced to the necessity of wearing sandals, made of raw hide.

On the 13th of December, the Twenty-seventh participated in the battle of Fredericksburg. After the battle of Fredericksburg, we went into winter quarters near Guinea's Station, and performed picket duty on the Rappahannock. On the 27th day of April, 1863, we took up the line of march for Chancellorsville, where we were engaged on the evening of the 29th, and again on the 30th at Wilderness Church, and again on the 1st day of May at Wilderness Tavern. Losing in the three engagements fifty-seven (57) men in killed and wounded. On the 4th day of May we returned to our old winter quarters, near Guinea's Station.

About the 19th of May the Twenty-seventh Georgia was ordered to report without delay to Major-General D. H. Hill, commanding the Department of North Carolina and Southern Virginia. The regiment arrived at Kinston, North Carolina, about the 28th of May and remained there until the 3d of July, when it was ordered back to Richmond to repel an anticipated raid of the enemy; arriving in Richmond on the 6th it only remained a few days, as it received orders to report at Wilmington, North Carolina, to General Whiting commanding that post. Upon the arrival of the regiment at Wilmington, it was immediately ordered to Topsail Sound, on the coast. Here the regiment remained until the 10th of August, when it was ordered to report to General Beauregard at Charleston, South Carolina, where it arrived on the 13th and marched to James Island. About the 28th of August we were ordered to Morris Island, where we remained until its evacuation, this regiment covering the retreat of the troops from the Island.

From September, 1863, until February, 1864, the Twenty-seventh remained on James Island doing picket duty there, and performing garrison duty at Fort Sumter. On the morning of the 12 of February the regiment marched for John's Island, where it arrived in time to assist General Wise in driving the enemy from their position on that Island.

On the 14th of February the Twenty-seventh, with the other regiments of Colquitt's Brigade, were ordered to Florida, and taking the cars on the Charleston and Savannah railroad it proceeded to Savannah, thence by the Atlantic and Gulf railroad to Valdosta, Georgia, where it arrived on the 15th. From Valdosta the regiment marched to Madison, Florida, and from thence by railroad to Olustee Station, on Tallahassee and Jackson railroad. During the early part of the day of the battle of Ocean Pond, the Twenty-seventh Georgia Regiment was held in reserve; but about four o'clock, P.M., it was ordered into the engagement, and immediately charging the enemy, contributed greatly to the utter rout and demoralization of the enemy. Colonel Zachry on this memorable occasion was termed the "*Blucher*" of the day. The loss of the Twenty-seventh Georgia in the battle of Ocean Pond, was very severe for the time it was engaged, amounting to eighty-seven (87) in killed and wounded. After the battle the enemy were pursued to Baldwin, Florida.

On the 1st day of March the Eleventh South Carolina, Twenty-seventh Georgia, and a force of cavalry, all under the command of Colonel Zachry, were ordered on a reconnoitering expedition. Near Cedar Creek they met with a force of the enemy, supposed to have been sent out for a similar purpose. After a short engagement the enemy were completely routed; and but for the failure of the cavalry to execute Colonel Zachry's orders, the entire party would have been captured. After the battles of Ocean Pond and Cedar Creek, the Twenty-seventh Georgia remained in camp, at Camp Milton, eight miles south of Baldwin, Florida, until the 19th of April, when it marched for Tebeauville, on the Atlantic and Gulf railroad. Arriving at that point they took cars, and proceeded by way of Savannah to Charleston, South Carolina. Upon arriving there it was ordered to James Island, where the regiment remained until May 11th, when it returned to Charleston, thence by railroad to Petersburg, Virginia, stopping, however, a few days at Weldon, North Carolina, in anticipation of a raid on that place. Arriving at Petersburg on the 19th, the Twenty-seventh was assigned a position on the front lines between the James and Appomattox rivers, where it remained until the 31st, when it was ordered to Cold Harbor. At the battle of Cold Harbor, on the 1st of June, five companies of this regiment charged and re-captured that portion of our lines lost by the left of General Clingman's Brigade. These five companies lost in the engagement, eleven (11) killed and fifty-four (54) wounded. The regiment remained on the front at Cold Harbor until the 13th of June, when it marched to Malvern Hill, leaving which place on the

14th, it marched to the vicinity of Richmond, where it remained until twelve o'clock, M., on the 15th, when the march was resumed to Chester Station, on the Richmond and Petersburg railroad, where it took the cars for Petersburg, where it arrived a little after dark, the same day.

The enemy having gained our works by assault before dark, the Twenty-seventh Georgia was assigned a position, and entrenched themselves during the night. On the night of the 17th of June the entire line was changed, and the Twenty-seventh Georgia was ordered to hold a very important salient, where they again entrenched themselves, as soon as it was possible so to do.

On the evening of the 18th of June, the enemy in three heavy columns, charged the position of this regiment. They were handsomely repulsed, with severe loss, over two hundred of their dead being left on the field. This salient was held by the Twenty-seventh Georgia regiment without any relief, until the 24th of June, with a loss of seventy-six (76) men killed and wounded. Among the wounded on the 18th was the gallant Lieutenant Colonel Gardner, who was mortally wounded, and died a few days thereafter. He was promoted to the position he held for distinguished gallantry, and his name and noble deeds will live forever embalmed in the hearts of his surviving comrades.

From the 24th of June until the 18th of August, this regiment was on the front, one-half of their time, alternating every three days, with a portion of General Martin's Brigade. On the 18th of August, while the Twenty-seventh Georgia was in reserve, the enemy advanced and took possession of the Weldon and Petersburg railroad, when the Twenty-seventh was ordered to the point attacked by the enemy, and engaged them on the evening of the same day. On the 19th this regiment formed a portion of a flanking party, who inflicted a heavy loss on the enemy in killed and wounded. Many prisoners were also taken.

The Twenty-seventh Georgia on this occasion, was under the command of Major H. Bussey. Owing to the natural features of the country, consisting as they did of thickly wooded spots, with a very dense undergrowth, it was impossible to preserve intact the advancing line of battle, large gaps would frequently be made in our lines, through which the enemy would make their way in detached parties, so that friend and foe would become thoroughly intermingled, and of necessity the fighting was very desperate, being sometimes almost hand to hand. It was an occasion which required great coolness and decision on the part of the commanding officers.

The whole regiment was several times in imminent danger of being captured, inspired however, by the unwavering coolness and intrepid valor of their leaders, these war-worn and battle-scarred veterans of many a bloody field would rally with enthusiasm around their tattered battle flag, and drive back with severe loss the advances of their assailants. A heavy rain having fallen a short time before the battle opened, and continuing to fall during its progress, the soil had become miry and slippery; the Twenty-seventh Georgia however, with other regiments of the brigade, making a gallant charge, drove the enemy with great slaughter from his entrenched line. Night put an end to the contest. The loss in killed and wounded in the Twenty-seventh Georgia was thirty, and twenty were taken prisoners. To compensate for this loss, besides the number of the enemy killed and wounded, a very large number of prisoners was taken; even the ambulance corps, in addition to attending to the wants of the wounded, captured eighty (80) prisoners.

At the present time, August 30th, 1864, the Twenty-seventh Georgia occupies an important position upon the defensive lines, around the city of Petersburg, Virginia.

Recapitulation of losses in the different battles in which the Twenty-seventh Georgia has been engaged:

Seven Pines,	killed and wounded, . . .	149
Battles around Richmond,	" " " . . .	126
Sharpsburg and South Mountain,	" " " . . .	154
Chancellorsville,	" " " . . .	57
Ocean Pond,	" " " . . .	87
Cold Harbor,	" " " . . .	65
Salient at Petersburg,	" " " . . .	76
On Weldon Railroad,	" " " . . .	30

Total casualties, ... 744
Loss in killed (as from statistical record), ... 104
Loss in wounded, ... 640

The losses in the regiment have certainly been severe. By adding to the real losses of the regiment, amounting to five hundred and forty-sex men, the number wounded six hundred and forty, we find that the losses of this regiment, like those of the Third, Sixth, and other Georgia regiments, *exceeds the total number of men enlisted and recruited*. This is explained by the fact that the only wounded men *lost* to the regiment, are those who have been discharged. Many of the men have also been wounded more than once.

THIRD REGIMENT

GEORGIA VOLUNTEERS

———

STATISTICAL RECORD.

Number of men originally enlisted, . .	932
Number of recruited, ...	551
Total, ...	1483

LOSSES IN EACH ENGAGEMENT.

Names of Battle.	Killed.	Wounded.	Died of wounds.
South Mills, April 12th, 1862,	5	12	2
Richmond, June 18th, 1862,	4	8	
King's School House, June 25th, 1862,	5	8	1
Malvern Hill, July 2d, 1862,	30	93	15
Rappahannock, August 25th, 1862,			
Manassas Number 2, August 30th, 1862,	3	26	1
Harper's Ferry, September 16th, 1862,			
Sharpsburg, September 17th, 1862,	20	67	4
Fredericksburg, December 13th, 1862,	1	1	
Chancellorsville, May 2d, 3d and 4th, 1863,	10	122	6
Gettysburg, July 2d, 1863,	29	141	15
Manassas Gap, July 23d, 1863,	12	37	
Wilderness, May 6th, 1864,	1	1	
Spottsylvania, May 14th, 1864,	11	73	9
Siege of Petersburg,	28	104	5
Total,	159	688	59

The losses by death are:–

Killed in action, ...	159
Died from wounds, ...	59
Died from disease, ...	213
Total, ...	431
Discharged and transferred, ...	342
Total loss from all causes, ...	773

The total of casualties is:–

Killed, ...	159
Wounded, ...	688
	847

The Third Georgia Regiment, composed of Volunteer companies who responded to the first call for troops to defend the integrity of the Confederate States, rendezvoused at Portsmouth, Virginia. At the Gosport Navy Yard, the regiment was organized by the election of the following officers: A. R. Wright of Augusta, Colonel; James S. Reid of Madison, Georgia, Lieutenant Colonel; and A. H. Lee of Covington, Georgia, Major. Lieutenant W. W. Turner, of Eatonton, Georgia, was appointed Adjutant; Captain H. S. Hughes received the appointment of Commisary, and Captain Alexander Phillips, Assistant Quartermaster of the regiment; and the Rev. Mr. Flinn of Milledgeville, was commissioned Chaplain.

The following companies composed the original organization of the regiment. With one or two exceptions, all were organized volunteer companies several years previous to the war.

Company A, Burke Guards, Burke County, Captain Charles Musgrove.
Company B, Brown Rifles, Putnam County, Captain Reuben B. Nisbet.
Company C, Dawson Grays, Green County, Captain Robert L. McWhorter.
Company D, Home Guards, Morgan County, Captain Charles H. Andrews.
Company E, Governor's Guards, Houston County, Captain Joel R. Griffin.
Company F, Wilkinson Rifles, Wilkinson County, Captain William O. Beall.
Company G, Confederate Light Guards, Richmond County, Captain Edward J. Walker.
Company H, Young Guards, Newton County, Captain John F. Jones.
Company I, Blodget Volunteers, Richmond County, Captain Foster Blodget.
Company K, Athens Guards, Clarke County, Captain Henry C. Billups.

In August, 1861, Captain Blodget's company was transferred from the regiment, and shortly afterwards the Clarke County Rifles, Captain Isaac S. Vincent, and the Carswell Guards, from Wilkinson County, Captain N. A. Carswell, were added to the regiment.

On the 29th of August, 1861, in pursuance of orders from Brigadier General, afterwards Major General, Huger, the Third Georgia embarked on small steamers and canal boats for the coast of North Carolina. Information being received on the way that Fort Hatteras had fallen, the Third Georgia was landed on Roanoke Island, and charged with the important duty of fortifying that position as speedily as possible, in order to prevent the further encroachments of the Yankees on the inland waters of North Carolina, and the approaches to the rear of Norfolk. The emergency was great, and the men comprehending it, worked with a will, night and day for several weeks, until formidable sand batteries, mounted with thirty-two pounders and columbiads bade defiance to Butler's fleet.

On the 1st of October three or four companies of this regiment embarked on two or three gunboats belonging to Commodore Lynch's fleet, and participated in the capture of the United States gunboat *Fanny*. The prize, with its cargo of provisions and clothing for the Twentieth Indiana Regiment, estimated to be worth one hundred thousand dollars, together with two pieces of field artillery and about forty prisoners, were the fruits of this combined movement of our little navy and the four companies above mentioned.

On the 4th of October all the companies of this regiment, about seven hundred strong, together with two companies of the Seventh North Carolina State Troops, and Colonel Shaw's Eighth North Carolina Regiment, went on board the gunboats and transport steamers constituting Commodore Lynch's "Mosquito Fleet," and sailed by night for the point where the *Fanny* had been captured. Arrived there, the camp of the enemy was discovered on the Chickamacomico banks, and we at once commenced a vigorous shelling. The enemy's camp was stampeded, the Hessians flying for their lives. They left behind them a smoking breakfast of poultry, coffee and various other luxuries. Their whole camp equipage, consisting of tents, cooking utensils, etc., all the officers' baggage, and ten days' rations of bacon, bread, sugar, coffee, &c., fell into our hands; all of which was successfully transported to our own camp on Roanoke Island.

The Third Georgia landed as soon as possible, wading in the water up to their cartridge boxes about one half mile, and immediately started in rapid pursuit of the Yankees. The latter having about two hours' start of us, the time occupied in landing troops, and proving exceedingly swift footed, kept out of our reach, and succeeded in gaining the light house, where they received reinforcements,–not escaping, however, without a loss of about forty prisoners, and the throwing away of nearly all their knapsacks and accoutrements, and the throwing into the sea of all the muskets belonging to their regiment.

On the 5th, the Third Georgia and two companies of the Seventh North Carolina, having chased the enemy a distance of twenty miles, returned to the place of landing. While returning along the ocean beach, the troops were shelled for several hours by the Federal sloop of war *Monticello*, but escaped without loss of life or casualties of any kind. After going through that arduous march, all safely returned on the 6th, to Roanoke Island, with a loss of but one man, who died from exhaustion on the march. The above detailed affair is well known as the "Chickamacomico races."

After completing the fortifications on Roanoke Island and building winter quarters,–the enemy in the meanwhile having been kept close to their conquest of the Hatteras sand banks,–our regiment was relieved by the Thirty-first North Carolina, Colonel Jordan, and returned to General Blanchard's Brigade station, around Portsmouth.

After the fall of Roanoke Island, the regiment was ordered to Elizabeth City, North Carolina, and remained in that vicinity for several months.

On the 19th of April, 1862, Colonel Wright, then in command of the forces around South Mills, learning of the landing of a large body of the Yankees prepared his troops (consisting of a few militia under Colonel Furribee, two companies of the Seventh North Carolina, Captain McComas' Virginia battery, and the Third Georgia) for battle. With this small force we met the enemy, and a battle was fought about two miles south of South Mills, which resulted in inflicting a heavy loss upon the enemy. We kept them back until nearly night, when our forces fell back into their entrenchments, and the enemy came upon the ground occupied by us in the morning. After night the enemy retreated to their gunboats, leaving their dead and part of their wounded in our hands. Considering the disparity of numbers engaged–the enemy's force consisting of three brigades of infantry, with two batteries of artillery, all under the command of Brigadier General Reno, while our force engaged scarcely numbered four hundred, and the whole force present amounting to but six hundred—the brilliancy of this affair is eclipsed by no achievement of the war. Our loss in killed, wounded, and missing, was fourteen, while that of the enemy is estimated at from four to five hundred.

On the 28th of April, 1862, the regiment was reorganized according to the provisions of the conscript act. But five of the old Captains were re-elected. Colonel A. R. Wright and Lieutenant-Colonel James S. Reid, were re-elected to their positions, and Lieutenant John R. Sturgis, of the Burke Guards, was elected Major.

About the time of the evacuation of Norfolk and Portsmouth, this command was ordered to Suffolk, and from there marched across the country to Petersburg; and just before the battle of Seven Pines, joined the Army of General Joseph E. Johnston. Though on the field and under fire, we did not become engaged in that battle.

During the month of June, we occupied a position on the extreme front line of the Chickahominy, on the Williamsburg road, being on picket duty or supporting the pickets the whole time. Besides many smaller engagements, we participated in a hot skirmish on the 18th of June, driving back a New Hampshire brigade with a considerable loss to them in killed and wounded, and about a dozen prisoners, while we lost two killed. On the 25th of the same month, we were called upon to repel a heavy advance of the enemy on our picket lines which crossed the Williamsburg road. Though under a heavy storm of grape and canister, we had not the opportunity of returning the fire. On this occasion we lost two killed and several severely wounded.

About the 3d of June Colonel A. R. Wright was promoted to be Brigadier General, leaving Major Sturgis commander of the Third Georgia, Lieutenant Colonel Reid having resigned about the same time. We participated in all the manoeuvres and marching of Wright's Brigade, Huger's Division, during the few days preceding the 1st of July, and on that day, with the other regiments composing the brigade, opened the fight at Malvern Hill. The Third Georgia was in the unsuccessful charge upon the enemies batteries, and lost heavily in officers and men. While they remained in the fight, holding the ground gained, until nine o'clock, P.M., our loss in killed was fifty-seven and in wounded ninety-four. Major John R. Sturgis was among the killed; he was a Christian gentleman, polished and courteous; he was also an efficient officer and generally very popular among his men and with his superior officers. As do the brave, he fell on the field of victory with his sword drawn in his country's cause. Captain

R. B. Nisbet, second in command, behaved gallantly and fearlessly upon this bloody field, and was severely wounded. We took into action about two hundred and fifty men, rank and file.

On the Chickahominy we suffered severely from disease. In one month our ranks were reduced, by sickness and the casualties of battle, from one thousand to about three hundred for duty. Soon after the battles around Richmond, we were left without field officers, and even without a Captain to take command. At this period Major N. B. Montgomery, P. A. C. S., was assigned to the command of the Third Georgia. Soon after the celebrated campaign against Pope commenced, in which this regiment participated, and in the laurels won in that campaign by Anderson's Division, this regiment claims a full share. At the second battle of Manassas we lost four killed and twenty-two wounded. Major Montgomery commanded in this engagement, and distinguished himself by his fearlessness on the field of battle. He received a severe wound, disabling him from command. At this time Captain Nisbet (then entitled, and soon after promoted, to the rank of Lieutenant Colonel) returned and assumed command of the regiment. The next important battle in which our regiment was engaged, was Sharpsburg. Here we took into action one hundred and twenty-five men, and lost twenty-four killed and forty-eight wounded. Lieutenant Colonel Nisbet commanded the regiment in this never to be forgotten battle, and after leading his command into line, fell dangerously wounded in several places. He was left on the field of battle and fell into the hands of the enemy. Captain John F. Jones succeeded to the command of the regiment. He was soon after promoted to Major, while Captain Edward J. Walker was made Colonel, and Captain R. B. Nisbet Lieutenant Colonel of the regiment. In the first battle of Fredericksburg, though present on the field and under a heavy fire, we did not become engaged with the enemy. We lost one man killed by a shell, Colonel Edward J. Walker, commanding.

During the months of January and February, 1863, Wright's Brigade was stationed at the United States Ford, on the Rappahannock. Fortifications were required, and the men worked day and night, through snow and rain, to complete them. The Third Georgia bore more than an equal share in these hardships. The sufferings of this command at United States Ford, from cold, short rations, and a scanty supply of clothing, could scarcely have been excelled by those which so severely tried the fortitude and patriotism of our forefathers, when quartered in the historic Valley Forge. Under command of Major Jones, the Third Georgia shared in all the marches and engagements around Chancellorsville and Fredericksburg during the first week in May. Major Jones received a wound at Chancellorsville which cost him his right arm. In a charge upon the Yankees around Donmond's house, near Fredericksburg, under the immediate observation of General Lee, the Third Georgia elicited the hearty praise of that soldier chieftain. Our loss in the several engagements was sixteen killed and one hundred and fifteen wounded.

The Third Georgia continued in Wright's Brigade, Anderson's Division, Hill's Corps, and participated largely in all the hardships and fighting of these organizations in the second invasion of the enemy's country by the Army of Northern Virginia.

The deeds of Wright's Brigade on the 2d of July, 1863, at the battle of Gettysburg, are already known to the public. It is but sufficient to say, that the Third Georgia merited a full share of the laurels won there. We carried into action five hundred men, and our losses were forty-one killed and one hundred and forty-eight wounded. Colonel Walker commanded in the battle of Gettysburg, and Captain C. H. Andrews acted as Lieutenant Colonel.

On the 23d of July, 1863, Wright's Brigade was ordered to guard the pass at Manassas Gap. The different corps of our army were marching through Front Royal and Chester Gap, and it was important to prevent the enemy from cutting our columns in two. This regiment was assigned to a position on the right of the brigade, and separated from it nearly a mile. Our position was on the top of a mountain, which commanded a view of the enemy's position. About two o'clock, P.M., the enemy having concentrated a force of about ten thousand men, advanced in solid column. Our command skirmished with them until numbers bore down too heavily, when we fell back to a position nearer the brigade. Here Captain Andrews, in obedience to orders to hold our position at all hazards, disposed of his forces properly, and calmly awaited the approach of the enemy. Soon their solid massive columns appeared over the mountain top, and they came pouring down upon us. When they arrived within three hundred yards, our Enfield rifles commenced fire upon them, and as they steadily advanced, our boys kept up a continuous fire, which often broke their ranks, and turned them back in confusion. But the fresh columns supporting their advance came on, until out-flanked and borne down by weight of numbers, our regiment was ordered to fall back to the supporting line behind us. The Yankees did not pursue, being checked by our artillery, which had by this time gotten into position. We had done heavy execution in the enemy's ranks, killing and wounding more than the total number of our regiment engaged; besides, our brigade thus held the enemy in check until Lieutenant General Ewell could bring up the troops of his corps, and get them into position to prevent their further advance. Colonel Edward J. Walker was in command of the brigade, and was badly wounded. The regiment numbered in this engagement about two hundred men, and lost in killed, fourteen, and in wounded, forty-five men. The brigade was highly complimented by Lieutenant General Ewell, who was on the field and witnessed its conduct. The troops in the line of battle supporting us, were on a hill which commanded a view of the combatants. They warmly congratulated their comrades of the Third Georgia upon their heroic conduct.

The enemy after a long season of quiet, suddenly exhibited signs of activity early in May, 1864.

On the 4th instant, the regiment, in conjunction with the Division of General Anderson, broke up camp and marched to Vediersville. A part of our cavalry force had already engaged the enemy and drove them back towards Chancellorsville. We continued on the road to a point known as Parker's Store, when the advance of our army became engaged, and fought during the rest of the day, and again on the next day.* These fights on the 5th and 6th of May, are well known as the battle of the Wilderness.

General Grant having failed in his direct assault, pursued his future movements by parallels, and the two armies again collided at Spottsylvania Court House. The Third Georgia was not actively engaged in the general engagements of either of the above named fights, but on the 14th instant at Spottsylvania, in connection with other forces, charged the Yankees in their breastworks, and after a fight of twenty minutes duration, routed them, capturing one stand of colors, and many small arms. Our loss was, for the length of time engaged, very severe, being seventy-eight men killed and wounded. Again the enemy moved; this time towards the North Anna river. During this movement, his rear was attacked by a portion of Anderson's Division, this regiment supporting Harris' Mississippi Brigade. The enemy were forced back upon the main column, but owing to the lateness of the hour, further active operations were suspended. Many minor incidents of interest occurred, but which space forbids mention of. The regiment after the incident mentioned

---

* I am assured that my informant (the Adjutant of the Third Georgia,) is mistaken in the dates of the battle of the Wilderness, and have changed them accordingly.

above marched to Petersburg. To detail all that has been done by Anderson's Division, which during the whole campaign has been commanded by General Mahone, and in which the Third Georgia has borne a conspicuous part, would occupy too great space.

The regiment took a part in the dreadful fight of July 30th, when Grant, by springing a mine under our works, succeeded in gaining foothold within our lines. The Third Georgia was in the desperate charge, (which resulted in the almost total annihilation of the Yankees and negroes, who were in our lines,) and lost heavily. In appreciation of the services of the division during the siege of Petersburg, General A. P. Hill has published the following congratulatory order, in which he expresses his admiration for the great services performed by the division:

HEADQUARTERS THIRD ARMY CORPS,
August 4th, 1864.

GENERAL ORDERS No. 17.

Anderson's Division, commanded by Brigadier General William Mahone, has so distinguished itself by it successes during the present campaign, as to merit the special mention of the corps commander; and he tenders to the division, its officers and men, his tanks for the gallantry displayed by them, whether in attacking or attacked.

Thirty-one (31) stand of colors, fifteen (15) pieces of artillery, and four thousand (4000) prisoners captured in battle, are the proud mementoes which signalize their valor, and entitle it to the admiration and gratitude of our country.

[Signed]

A. P. HILL, Lieutenant General.

Of the above three stand of colors, many prisoners and part of a battery of artillery, show what part the Third regiment has taken in the conflicts of the campaign, while its long list of killed and wounded sufficiently attest its gallantry. The fight of July 30th was the last engagement in which the Third Georgia has borne a part up to the present time of writing, (August 4th.) The instances of personal bravery have been so numerous that commanders dislike to make distinctions, in giving names to the public. A few are, however, appended.

In the charge at Gettysburg, while the regiment was driving the enemy before them, the color-bearer was shot down and the battle flag fell to the ground. Adjutant Samuel L. Alexander, being near by snatched up the colors and bore them aloft, as the regiment advanced triumphantly to the guns of the enemy. While carrying the colors Adjutant Alexander had his uniform pierced by eight bullets, and was severely wounded in the right arm.

The day after the battle of Manassas, No. 2, Lieutenant John H. Evans, of Covington, then but a mere boy in years, was wandering over the battle field, when he came suddenly upon a picket of the enemy, consisting of thirty (30) men, who in the hurry of the flight, the day previous, had not been relieved. Not at all abashed by the number of the enemy, he coolly ordered them to surrender, and marched them triumphantly to the rear.

After leaving the Chickamacomico beach, it was discovered, upon our return to Roanoke Island, that one poor youth was missing, having been when last seen, delirious and idiotic from excessive fatigue. Colonel Wright called for a volunteer to go in search of him. Private Rice, of company H, stepped forward and offered his services which were accepted. Securing a small skiff, he recrossed the Albemarle Sound, landed on the beach then reoccupied by the Yankees, and after several days' absence and many adventures, returned to Roanoke Island, bringing in safety his lost friend. And thus instance after instance might be related of individual gallantry and devotion, enough to fill a volume; and it is easier to mention the few who have not behaved well, than the many who have on all occasions and under all circumstances, sustained so nobly their own and their regiment's widely known renown.

Not a field officer who has ever commanded in action has escaped. General A. R. Wright, late Colonel of the Third Georgia, has been twice wounded. Major Sturgis was killed; Major Montgomery wounded; Colonel Walker wounded; Lieutenant Colonel Nisbet has been wounded time and again; Major Jones also severely wounded. Company A has had three officers killed or maimed for life, and two wounded twice. Company B of Putnam has had thirteen men killed and eighty-eight wounded. Company F, of Wilkinson, has had twenty-two killed and seventy-two wounded. In a word, the Third Georgia, or the "old Third," as it is called in Anderson's Division, is one of the historic regiments of our State, and needs no laudation, as its gallant deeds are entwined around the hearts of a grateful people. Like the Fourth, Sixth, Seventh, Eighth, Twelfth, Fourteenth and Eighteenth and other of the first volunteer regiments in the Army of Northern Virginia, it has made for itself an imperishable renown, and decked its banners with unfading laurels. And to-day she holds her place on the right of Wright's Brigade, five hundred strong, despite the grape, canister and minie balls, despite the frequent presence of the grim monster Death, ready to enter upon another campaign with a courage as high, an enthusiasm as noble, as she exhibited upon the 1st of May, 1861, when she marched from the city of Augusta, near one thousand strong, on her route to the glorious Old Dominion, with drums beating and banners flying, over a host of as brave hearts and strong arms as ever offered themselves as modern "Macarias" upon the sacrificial altars of their country.

The following resolution was adopted unanimously by the last Congress:–

"*Joint Resolution of thanks to the Officers and Men of the Third Georgia Regiment.*

"Resolved by the Congress of the Confederate States of America,–That the thanks of Congress are due, and are hereby tendered to the officers and men of the Third Georgia Regiment, through its representatives in Congress, who were the first to leave their state to battle on the soil of Virginia; whose gallant dead have been left on many of her historic battle-fields; which entire regiment, to a man, has cheerfully and unanimously re-enlisted for the war,–resolving that as they were the first to take up arms in the cause of liberty and independence, they will be the last to lay them down.

"Approved February 15th, 1864."

Thus hurriedly and incompletely has been thrown together a few of the prominent facts connected with the history of this regiment,–hoping that when peace shall again smile upon us, you may be enabled to collect from the remnant of its war-worn veterans, materials to fill a niche in a full and complete history of the volunteer soldiery of the Empire State of the South.

Connected with this regiment are two or three incidents which I have gathered *outside* of the foregoing report, and I am constrained to notice them.

A GALLANT LIEUTENANT.

During one of our fights with the enemy near Spottsylvania Court House, Virginia, on the 14th of May, General Wright's Brigade was ordered to charge the enemy's works. In doing so the Third Georgia passed through a heavy fire of minie balls, losing seventy-eight men in killed and wounded. The color-bearer of the regiment being wounded, planted the colors in the ground and retired to the rear. At this moment the skirmish line was ordered to halt, which was understood by many as an order for the regiment to halt, which they did. Perceiving that a crisis was at hand, Lieutenant R. G. Hyman sprang forward, seized the colors from amid a pile of the slain, and waving the cross of our country in the face of the foe, called upon the old Third to rally to it, which they did with a rebel yell, and the Yankee breastworks were taken. Lieutenant Hyman was at least fifty yards in advance of the regiment all the time. He has been highly complimented by Lieutenant General Hill and all his officers; he is of Company F, of Wilkinson County, Georgia.

Color-sergeant Livingston of Company C, was killed while bearing the colors at least thirty yards in front of his regiment. His gallantry was particularly conspicuous, and his name deserves to be placed high in the list of the "Heroes and Martyrs" of our native state.

The original color guard of ten men of this regiment, have all been killed in battle, excepting E. R. Hughes of Wilkinson County, and his life would doubtless have been lost, had it not been for the ball striking two brass checks in his pocket. As it was, he was severely wounded.

In closing this list, I cannot forbear mentioning the name of the brave but unfortunate Lieutenant Colonel R. B. Nisbet, whose name is almost a by-word in his brigade, for coolness, courage, and unexcelled bravery. At Sharpsburg he received seven very severe wounds, any of which might have proven fatal. He was severely wounded at Malvern Hill also. He is now placed on the retired list, but his burning spirit is still eager for the fray. His many honorable scars point to him the necessity of his remaining in quiet, but the bugle notes of his gallant comrades' battle shout, arouse the lion within him, and his soul pants to lead them on to victory in his country's cause.

There appears a wide disparity between the report of casualties by the Adjutant, and the report furnished me by a member of the regiment, revised and corrected by Colonel Nisbet himself. According to the information I have gained by enquiry among the company commanders, &c., the losses of the Third Georgia in killed and wounded, stand as follows:–

Killed in action, ...	221
Wounded, ...	<u>667</u>
Total of casualties, ...	888

Company F, of Wilkinson County, according to the report of the Adjutant, has lost twenty-two (22) men killed: but Captain Mason, its commander, assures me that he has lost thirty-one (31) men killed. I am informed that the cause of the difference in the two reports, is that the Adjutant's book has been once or twice lost, and that the error, therefore, lies in his report; also that there have been several incumbents of the adjutancy, and that an error in the report of the present incumbent, is likely to arise through no fault on his part.

GEORGIA VOLUNTEERS

———

STATISTICAL REPORT.

Number of men originally enlisted, ...	854
Number of recruits received, ...	241
Number of conscripts, ...	33
Total, ...	1128

LOSSES.

Number of men killed in action, ...	189
Number of men died of wounds and disease, ...	261
Total of deaths, ...	450
Number of men discharged, ...	102
Number of men deserted; (substitutes, all), ...	19
Total real losses, ...	571
Number of men wounded in battle, ...	353
Total of real and apparent loss, ...	929

CHANGES IN FIELD OFFICERS.

Major J. R. Whitehead resigned July 17th, 1863; the vacancy was filled by the promotion of Captain M. R. Hall. Lieutenant Colonel R. W. Carswell resigned December 23d, 1863, and the vacancy was filled by the promotion of Major M. R. Hall. The regiment has no Major at present. Captain A. C. Flanders will no doubt receive the appointment of Major. The regiment is composed of ten companies, as follows:–

ORIGINAL ORGANIZATION.

Company A, Gibson Volunteers, Glasscock County, Captain A. Kelley.
Company B, Warren Infantry, Warren County, Captain M. R. Hall.
Company C, Georgia Light Guards, Richmond County, Captain H. S. Dortic.
Company D, Burke Volunteers, Burke County, Captain J. A. Harlow.
Company E, Jefferson Volunteers, Jefferson County, Captain R. W. Carswell.
Company F, Battle Ground Guards, Johnson County, Captain T. W. Kent.
Company G, Slappey Guards, Twiggs County, Captain U. A. Rice.
Company H, McLeod Volunteers, Emanuel County, Captain Neal McLeod.
Company I, Wilson Tigers, Richmond County, Captain R. J. Wilson.
Company K, Hamilton Rangers, Columbia County, Captain T. J. Hamilton.

The companies assembled at Camp Davis, in Effingham County, Georgia, on the 10th and 11 days of March, 1862. On the 15th the regiment was organized and field officers were elected. William Gibson, a private in the company from Richmond County, was unanimously chosen Colonel; Captain R. W. Carswell, of Jefferson County, was also unanimously elected Lieutenant Colonel; and J. Randolph Whitehead was, by a majority vote, elected Major.

On the 17th of March the regiment was ordered to Grahamsville, South Carolina. They proceeded to that point by railroad, their baggage requiring more cars to transport it, than were occupied by the troops. During the stay of the regiment at Grahamsville, the alarm was sounded one night about midnight, and the regiment was gotten under arms and double-quicked about three miles towards the coast to meet the Yankees, "reported" to be advancing from that direction. Every one was kept in the dark, except the field officers, until the *stimulus* was exhausted, and the getters-up of the alarm had to return to camp to get a fresh supply of hoaxing material. The boys returned to camp very much fatigued, satisfied to let the "powers that be" enjoy their joke, so long as their slumbers were not again disturbed.

The regiment left Grahamsville, on the 5th of May, for Charleston, and reached their destination the next day. The regiment made a great display as they marched through the streets of the city in all their pristine strength; but, alas! where are they now? Many of them are lying beneath the consecrated soil of Virginia, with no tablet to mark their last resting place! Many, the maimed and scarred victims of this hellish war, are lingering out lives of agony at home! But the few that are left–the glorious, gallant few–are still standing, proudly hurling defiance at the foe! The regiment was camped in Hampstead Mall, near Half Moon Battery, which was a very gay place for soldiers–no duty to perform except guard duty, (which the boys thought very hard), and occasionally battalion drill. Rations were very good; vegetables and fresh meats abounded in the market, and money was very plentiful with all the boys, as they had just received their fifty dollars bounty; but this was too good to last long. The regiment was dissatisfied, as soldiers usually are, when they have nothing to do, and they were very anxious to get into more active service.

On the 25th of May the regiment was ordered to Richmond, Virginia. It left Charleston one thousand strong, carrying sixteen (16) cars loaded with baggage. The troops were compelled to lay over two days in Wilmington, for want of transportation. June 2d the regiment arrived in Richmond, and were ordered into camp, near the suburbs of the city, on the Williamsburg road, where they remained until the commencement of the battles around Richmond.

On the 25th of June, 1862, at one o'clock, A.M., the regiment was ordered under arms, and marched to Chancellorsville, where it arrived about the middle of the day. It was allowed to rest until late in the evening, and was then moved across the Chickahominy river, and formed in line of battle to assault the enemy's works. Ripley's Brigade, to which the Forty-eighth Georgia was attached, was ordered to charge the enemy's line of entrenchments, distant from us about one mile. The troops moved forward with great spirit and zeal, as though they expected an easy job. On nearing the works, the enemy opened upon us with artillery; the line pressed forward, and very soon the sharp crack of musketry told that "the Angel of Death had spread his wings on the blast." It was getting dark and the distance could not be calculated. The troops continued to advance under the heavy fire of infantry and artillery, without faltering, until they came to an impassable canal or millrace, within two hundred yards of the enemy's works, that could not by any means be passed, and the regiment was ordered to fall back a short distance, and hold the ground they had gained. The troops were withdrawn in good order, and their line established in the edge of a pine thicket, about four hundred yards from the enemy's works, where they remained until morning. Losses of the Forty-eighth Georgia, ten killed and twenty-five wounded.

On the 27th of June the regiment left Mechanicsville for Cold Harbor, and arrived there about three o'clock, P.M. The march was a very hard one, and the weather very warm. The nights were very cool, and the men suffered much for want of covering to shield them from the cold night air, as they were brought from camp in light marching order, without knapsacks or blankets.

The brigade was not engaged in the battle of Cold Harbor, they being held in reserve; but so close to the engagement were they, that several men were killed and wounded in the Forty-eighth Georgia. The troops had made a forced march to get there, but were in good spirits, and ready for any work they might have been called upon to do. The loss was four killed and five wounded.

The 28th and 29th days of June, we remained on the battle field, caring for the wounded, burying the dead, and gathering up arms, sutler's stores, &c., left on the field by the enemy in their hot haste to get away.

On the 30th of June, the Forty-eighth followed the enemy to White Oak Swamp, and there camped for the night. The next morning (July 1st,) early, we started to Malvern Hill, and arrived there about three o'clock in the evening. The brigade was formed into line, and about six o'clock was ordered into the fight, to support some troops in front of us. Owing to some misunderstanding of the orders, Colonel Gibson moved up only two companies, the other eight companies remaining behind in a ravine with Lieutenant Colonel Carswell. When the battle was nearly over the mistake was discovered, and the balance of the regiment was brought up, but too late to get into the fight. The two companies engaged, displayed great coolness under fire, and delivered *their* fire with great effect upon the enemy. Losses four killed and thirty-nine wounded.

In this engagement Colonel Gibson had one ball to pass through his coat, and another to cut away the top of a low felt hat he was wearing.

The next day the regiment was moved from the battle field about two miles, and ordered into camp, where we remained about a week, and then returned to the old camp near Richmond.

The day after our arrival at our old camp, the regiment was transferred to the brigade of General A. R. Wright, of Augusta,

Georgia, and in a few days moved to Falling Creek, where the brigade was at that time encamped. While at this camp the men were very sickly, numbers of them dying daily. Some companies numbering over one hundred men, had only twenty, and twenty-five men fit for duty.

About the 1st day of August the regiment was moved to Point of Rocks, on the Appomattox river, distant from Falling Creek twelve miles. While there the health of the men improved considerably.

On the 16th of August the command returned to Falling Creek, and on the 18th started to the Valley after Pope, whose headquarters were at that time in the saddle, but which were soon superseded by other quarters. The march to Manassas was one which severely tried the patience of the men. They were often without any thing to eat, except green corn and apples. Many of them were barefooted and nearly naked. On the 28th of August the regiment had a skirmish with the enemy, near Jefferson, Virginia, losing two men wounded. From Jefferson the regiment went on to Manassas, where they arrived about five o'clock, A.M. They formed line and rested until evening. The fight was raging with great fury when they were ordered in. The Forty-eighth Georgia was marching through a thick piece of woods, where they came upon the enemy in ambush. They poured a volley into our ranks before our men were aware that they were near an enemy. The fire was received with great coolness, and they at once returned the fire, and in a few minutes had the Yankees flying for safety, leaving many dead and wounded in our hands. Our loss was, killed twenty-two (22), wounded twenty-eight (28). In this engagement the men and officers displayed great gallantry and did vast execution.

Here fell the brave and noble Captain Allen Kelley, mortally wounded. Although a member of the Georgia Legislature and subject to neither conscription or draft, he gave his services to his country, and nobly fell battling for its freedom and independence. After one of his men had fallen, he seized his gun and pressed forward, giving his commands and assisting in their execution, until he himself was lain bleeding and mortally wounded, upon the sod. He was idolized by his brave boys, and highly esteemed by his brother officers of the line, and implicitly confided in by his superior officers, for his cool and dauntless courage and great discretion, at all times and under all circumstances. Here also Colonel Gibson received a painful wound, but did not quit the field until the fighting had ceased. He returned, however, on the very next morning.

From Manassas the regiment went into Maryland, crossing the Potomac at Leesburg, September 3d. From Leesburg it proceeded to Frederick City, Maryland, where it remained three days, and then to Maryland Heights near Harper's Ferry. The Forty-eighth remained there until its capitulation, which occurred on Monday, September 16th. On the evening of the 15th, it recrossed at Harper's Ferry, moved up the river towards Sharpsburg, and at eight o'clock, A. M. on the 17th, crossed the Potomac at Shepherdstown, marched about two miles, formed line, and rested about fifteen minutes. Knapsacks were thrown off, and the troops ordered forward at the expiration of that time. The brigade advanced about eight hundred yards under a heavy artillery fire, when they came upon the enemy's line of infantry. The ground was hotly contested for three hours, resulting in a drawn battle. The Forty-eighth charged them several times, and would succeed in driving them back, but were compelled each time to fall back, by the large numbers of fresh troops they would bring against us. At this fight Colonel Gibson was slightly wounded in two places.

The regiment remained in line all that day and the day following, until at twelve o'clock at night orders were given to withdraw from the field and cross the river at Shepherdstown; which was done in good order. Losses in the Forty-eighth at Sharpsburg amounted to, killed twenty-one, wounded thirty-six. After crossing the river we marched about three miles east of Shepherdstown, and formed line, expecting the enemy to follow us. After remaining in line the day and no enemy appearing, we were marched to a point near Martinsburg, and bivouacked until the 25th of September. We then started for Winchester, and after one of the most tiresome night marches that men ever endured, reached Winchester at about four o'clock, A.M., when we struck camp, and remained until the 1st of November. While at this point, man and beast fared well. Fine water, fine beef and pork were plentiful. November 1st the troops left Winchester for Culpepper, and marched that day twenty-three miles. At night the boys were so broken down, that only nineteen of the regiment came up to stack arms. The next morning at seven o'clock the boys had all come up, ready for another day's march. We reached Culpepper on the 3d of November, and remained until the 20th. While at this camp an amusing circumstance occurred with a fellow in the Quartermaster's Department. One of the men had got hold of a clock weight and fixed an artillery fuse to it, and carried it to the fire where several of the boys were standing, among them this Quartermaster gentleman, who was not accustomed to shells and had no desire to have them about him. He at once commenced persuading our waggish boy to throw it away, as it was very dangerous with the fuse attached. The man who had the weight, told him he wanted to see if it would burn, and thrust the fuse into the fire. As the fuse commenced to burn, the Quartermaster broke for dear life, running over a tent and through a large brush pile, swearing as he absquatulated, that he would shoot the next man that threw a shell into that fire.

On the 20th the regiment started for Fredericksburg, and arrived there on the 22d. On the 11th day of December, we formed line of battle near the town, and remained until the battle was over without participating, as the enemy did not advance upon us. After the fight was over we returned to camp, where we remained a few days only, as soon after our arrival we were ordered to United States Ford, where our sufferings were greater than men can usually endure. The Forty-eighth remained here from the 8th of January, 1863, until the 25th of February, without any tents or shelter, except such as the men could improvise with their blankets, &c., and even they were scarce. Rations were very poor, and very often the men had nothing to eat at all. The weather was very cold, the ground covered with snow and ice nearly all the time. A portion of our time was occupied in working on batteries that have never benefited us at all.

On the 25th of February, 1863, we started for camp near Guinea's Station. The snow was about eighteen inches deep, and very bad, of course, to travel through. That night we camped near Fredericksburg. The next morning it was raining, and the marching we did that day was awful. The ice, snow and mud were nearly knee deep, and the weather was extremely cold. We arrived at camp about three o'clock, P.M., and at once set about making fires to warm our frozen limbs. This camp was the winter quarters of General Hood's Division, and he had left them and gone below Petersburg. The little huts were neatly constructed and comfortable; wood was convenient and plentiful. The Forty-eighth remained at this camp until ordered to Chancellorsville to meet the army of "Fighting Joe Hooker."

On the 1st day of May we had a hot skirmish with a party of the enemy who were annoying Stuart's cavalry, and drove them back about one mile. That night we returned to the plank road east of the town, and remained there that day. The next morning we moved up nearer the town, fronting the enemy's works on the south side, and were the recipients of the most awful shelling ever witnessed. The next day the regiment went back to Fredericksburg, and charged the enemy's lines at Dounwan's House, completely routing them.

Regiment lost at Chancellorsville, eleven killed and twenty-seven wounded; at Dounwan's House, one killed and eight wounded. At the battle of Chancellorsville, Captain W. A. Kendrick of Twiggs County, the successor of Captain Rice, fell mortally wounded, and soon died. Captain Kendrick went into the ranks of the Forty-eighth Georgia as a private soldier, and was only about nineteen years of age; but such was his gallantry on every field, and such his gentlemanly deportment in camp, as marked him as a young man of no ordinary qualities; and upon the first vacancy occurring in his command he was elected by his company, first a lieutenant, and was afterwards promptly promoted to the command of his company.

In a few days the regiment was ordered back to their huts near Guinea's Station, and remained there until the army started to Pennsylvania. On the 4th of June the regiment went to Fredericksburg, and took position in the rifle pits surrounding that town. A little skirmish took place here, in which the Forty-eighth Georgia lost two men wounded. On the 14th of June the Forty-eighth started *for* Pennsylvania. The first two days' marches were very hard upon the boys, the weather being very hot and the rate of march too rapid, (twenty miles per day). Numbers of them fainted on the way, but soon recovered and followed on. The march *in* Pennsylvania was very pleasant and admirably conducted, making on an average about twelve miles per day. Gettysburg, the town which gave name to one of the most fearful battles of modern times, was reached July 1st, about five o'clock, P.M.

The next morning the line was formed, and at four o'clock, P.M., the most gallant charge ever executed by any troops, was made. The enemy's position was carried, but supports failing to make their appearance, we were compelled to retire, leaving many of our dead and wounded in the hands of the enemy. We then returned to our original line, and remained there until the night of the 4th. The loss of the Forty-eighth Georgia in this terrible battle, was fearful, amounting to eighty-one killed, and one hundred and twenty-five wounded. Three hundred and twenty-five men were all that were carried into action.

In this action Colonel Gibson fell severely wounded by three different balls, and was left on the field. The Lieutenant Colonel was wounded, the acting Major, Captain J. H. Harlow,[*] killed, and in fact, every officer of the line, except one captain and one lieutenant, was

---

[*] Colonel Gibson pays an eloquent tribute to the memory of this gallant officer, whose natural bravery could not be surpassed.

either killed or wounded. Captain T. H. Polhill, a brave, noble officer, fell. He was a young lawyer of much promise in his profession, a perfect gentleman and a good scholar. Captain Jarvis, a worthy successor of the gallant Kendrick, also poured out his blood upon this bloody field. The fearlessly brave Lieutenant Burnsides, in command of the company from the county of Columbia, also offered up his life upon the altar of his country. Captain Dick Wilson lost his arm; the undaunted Captain Kent fell severely wounded on the field; also Lieutenants Frank Allen, and Skinner, from Burke, were wounded.

On the night of the 4th the regiment commenced their retreat, which was conducted leisurely, the enemy not interfering. At Waynesboro, Pennsylvania, the Forty-eighth remained two days and made a capture of some horses and fifteen barrels of whisky, which, the weather being very inclement, was freely issued to the men, who had a very merry time, considering what a terrible ordeal they had but just passed through. It was assuredly a most welcome treat. At Hagerstown we halted for several days, and offered battle, but the enemy would not accept the proffered guantlet. On the night of the 10th of July we left Hagerstown, and marched to the Potomac. The night was very dark and the rain was falling heavily; the mud was very slippery, and but few men escaped a fall into it that night. The next morning the boys looked like they had been wallowing or laying at full length in the mud, which amusing spectacle was received at light with shouts of laughter. That morning, the 11th, we crossed the river at Falling Waters, rested there until the next day, and then marched to Bunker Hill. Here we remained a few days, and then went on to Front Royal.

On the 23d Wright's Brigade was sent to Manassas Gap to guard the mountain pass, until the army could effect its passage by Front Royal. We had been there but a few hours when the enemy's line advanced and drove in our skirmishers, and very soon engaged our line. The Yankee force on this occasion amounted to ten thousand men; our force did not exceed six hundred. We held them in check until General Ewell sent up reinforcements. We fought them three hours, and when General Ewell sent the supports, the Forty-eighth Georgia had but one round of ammunition. They poured that into the Yankees, and then retired to the line of supports. We returned that night to Front Royal and obtained some whisky, which our efficient Commissary had procured for us to revive our drooping spirits. We then turned toward Culpepper, and had a very pleasant time on the road for three days, the time required to get to our destination. We remained at Culpepper several days. On the 1st of August the Yankee cavalry came too near us, and we gave them a chase, but they ran too fast, and we could not overtake them. On the 3d of August we started for Orange Court House, and arrived there on the 4th. A month was spent at Orange very pleasantly.

On the 10th of September the Yankees advanced to the Rapid Ann river, and we were ordered to Robertson's Ford, three miles below the railroad bridge, to prevent the enemy from crossing. We remained there until the 8th day of October, when we started on a flank movement. That day we went to Burnett's Ford; the next day, to Madison Court House; the next, about six miles west of Culpepper; the next, to Warrenton; and the next, to Bristow Station, where we remained two days, and then returned to Culpepper. Here we remained until about the middle of November, and then returned to Rapid Ann Station. On the 28th of November General Meade crossed the river some distance below us, and we were sent to Mine Run to meet him. We had a light skirmish with them at this place, losing two killed and three wounded. While there we suffered very much from the excessive cold. We were compelled to remain in the trenches with very little fire, and the weather continued bitter cold. The Yankees would not accept battle, but retreated across the river, and we returned to our quarters at Rapid Ann Station, where we remained until the 27th, when the regiment was moved to Madison River Station, and there built very comfortable winter quarters, where we stayed and enjoyed ourselves finely until the spring campaign opened.

On the 29th of December, 1863, the regiment was ordered to build winter quarters, which was promptly done, and the men were soon sheltered (on Madison river). Here we remained until the middle of February, when we marched to meet the enemy advancing on Charlottesville. We arrived at Gordonsville about nine, P.M. From there Lieutenant Colonel Hall with the Forty-eighth Georgia and Second Georgia Battalion, was ordered to Frederick Hall to meet a raiding party; but the enemy had passed without doing any damage, before our arrival. Here we remained two days and then rejoined the brigade at Gordonsville. On the 4th of May we broke up camp and moved near Rapid Ann railroad bridge, and from thence proceeded to the Wilderness, and were held in reserve during the battle. When the army moved to Spottsylvania, we were left on the line, Wright's Brigade being in the rear of the army. A force of the enemy's cavalry being discovered trying to cross the Po river to intercept our wagon train, the Forty-eighth and Second Battalion, under Colonel Hall, were left to support our cavalry until the train passed. They then rejoined the brigade on the extreme right of the army, and took position. After night we moved back to the extreme left, to meet the advance of the enemy upon our left. Early in the morning they appeared in our front, and we had a spirited skirmish lasting half an hour, when the enemy retired, leaving several dead on the field; we lost none.

On the 14th of May the brigade attacked the enemy on their extreme left, driving them from their works and completely routing them. In this engagement the Forty-eighth Georgia acted well its part, capturing one stand of colors and several prisoners,–losing three killed and twenty-six wounded. We were next engaged at Hanover Junction, where for several days we kept up a regular sharp-shooting fight. From here we marched to Atlee's Station, arriving May 25th. While here Colonel Gibson rejoined his command, having been absent since the battle of Gettysburg, where he was wounded and taken prisoner.

Grant continuing his move by the left flank, we were ordered to Turkey Ridge, arriving there June 2d, and were put into position in the rear of Colquitt's Brigade, as supports, remaining there twenty-four hours, and then moved further to the right and took position in the front. At this point the lines of the opposing forces were but a hundred and seventy-five yards apart. Sharpshooting was kept up continually, causing the loss of some of our bravest men. From Turkey Ridge we moved to Riddle's Shop, fourteen miles from Richmond, and engaged the enemy on the 13th of June, commanded by Lieutenant Colonel Hall. The regiment was deployed and moved forward at once. Finding the enemy posted in an open field, with infantry, cavalry and three pieces of artillery, we attacked them and drove them from the field, leaving their dead in our hands. Our loss was four killed and thirteen wounded. This was a very creditable affair, as the enemy outnumbered us three to one. On the 22d of June Wright's Brigade attacked the enemy in their works near Petersburg, and with two other brigades captured their works, inflicting heavy loss in killed and wounded, besides capturing seventeen hundred prisoners. In this engagement the Forty-eighth made a gallant charge on the enemy's works under a most galling fire ever endured by men; but they pressed forward with cool courage until they gained the enemy's works. The loss of the Forty-eighth Georgia amounted to thirty killed and wounded.

On the next day, June 23d, we moved around the enemy's flank on the Weldon railroad. When we had arrived on the enemy's extreme left, their sharp-shooters commenced annoying us considerably. Colonel Hall was ordered to take the Forty-eighth and Second Battalion, and drive them from an elevated point in the woods. He quickly moved upon their flank and attacked them, killing, wounding and capturing nearly every man of them. He captured more than his own strength amounted to. The fighting was desperate,–nearly hand to hand. Some of our boys were shot within ten feet of the enemy, who paid dearly for their stubbornness; their loss being over two hundred, while ours was eleven wounded, three mortally. We here captured the colors of the Eighty-seventh Pennsylvania Regiment. Upon its arrival at Petersburg, the men from marching and two days' fighting, were worn out.

On the 30th of July, after the explosion of Grant's mine and the capture of a portion of our works, we were ordered there to assist in retaking the line. We arrived at the scene of the explosion about nine o'clock, A.M., and went into the fight on the right of Mahone's Brigade. The bullets whistled by us here faster than any man in the brigade ever heard before, and it was certainly one of the most sanguinary fights on record. Nothing could withstand the desperate valor of our boys, and we occupied the works on Mahone's immediate right, keeping up a continuous fire on the enemy until the whole line was re-established. In our front the dead lay thicker than has been seen on any battle-field of this war. The loss of the Forty-eighth was thirty-five killed and wounded. The battle-flag of the regiment was pierced by one hundred and three bullets, and three times was the staff cut in two in this engagement. The men and officers deserve great credit for their gallantry displayed here.

Tenth Battalion

GEORGIA VOLUNTEERS

———

Statistical Report.

Original strength, ...	346
Recruits, to August 1st, 1864, ...	293
Conscripts, ...	2
Total, ...	641

Losses by Death.

Killed in battle, ...	34
Died of disease, ...	156
Total of deaths, ...	190

Losses Otherwise Than by Death.

Discharged, ...	48
Deserted, ...	15
Transferred, ...	4
Resigned, ...	5
Cashiered, ...	1
Prisoner of war, ...	1
Total, ...	74
Total of actual losses, ...	264
Wounded in action, ...	118
Actual and temporary losses, . .	382

Number of substitutes in the battalion, ...   55
Present aggregate strength of the battalion, . .   378

The Tenth Battalion of Georgia Volunteers was organized at Camp Stephens, Georgia, on the 17th day of March, 1862, by the election of Captain John E. Rylander as Major. The battalion then consisted of the following four companies:–

Company A, Macon County Guards, Macon County, Captain J. D. Frederick.
Company B, Worth Rebels, Worth County, Captain Daniel Henderson.
Company C, Zollicoffer Rifles, Sumter County, Captain B. F. Bell.
Company D, Whittle Guards, Bibb County, Captain W. L. Jones.

By order of Brigadier General Mercer, commanding Department of Georgia, a fifth company was formed on the 17th of July, and John L. Adderton was elected to the Captaincy. The battalion remained at Camp Stephens until the 14th of May, 1862. While at this place it was most thoroughly drilled by Major Rylander.

At the expiration of the above mentioned time, it was ordered to Macon for the purpose of guarding several thousand Federal prisoners, confined at Camp Oglethorpe, near that city. At this most laborious and disgusting service, the battalion suffered exceedingly with sickness, and was not relieved until the last Federal prisoner was sent to Richmond to be exchanged. On the 15th of December, 1862, orders were received for the Battalion to proceed to Virginia, to join General Lee's army at Fredericksburg, Virginia. Arriving there on the 27th, it was attached to General G. T. Anderson's Brigade, General Hood's Division, Longstreet's Corps.

On the 17th of February, 1863, on the march from Fredericksburg to Richmond, with the rest of the army, it suffered incredible hardships, and for five days was exposed to all the horrors of a Northern Virginian snow storm, without any shelter whatever from the bitter blast, which blew cold o'er that, now almost desolated region. The Tenth Battalion participated in the campaign against Suffolk, and near its close was exchanged for the Fifty-ninth Georgia regiment, and was ordered thence to Fort Powhattan, on the James river. This important position was held under the most trying circumstances, by the Tenth Battalion for nearly two months.

At this time the enemy having apparently matured his plans for attacking the fort, by both land and water with vastly superior force. General D. H. Hill ordered the evacuation of the fort, the battalion falling back to Petersburg. About the middle of August, the enemy having made some daring demonstrations upon the Blackwater line, the battalion was ordered to Franklin. For eight months it held this line, protecting the surrounding country from the hostile incursions of the enemy, with entire satisfaction to the commandant of the department. About the 25th of April, 1864, it was ordered to report to General Lee, at Orange Court House, Virginia. Immediately upon its arrival at this place it was assigned to the brigade of General A. R. Wright, Anderson's Division, A. P. Hill's Corps. In connection with this division and brigade, the Tenth Battalion participated more or less in all the fierce battles and fatiguing marches of this memorable campaign. It gained no little credit for itself, in the desperate charge upon the fortified position of the enemy on the 14th of May, at Spottsylvania Court House.

On the 2d of June it had the misfortune to lose its most efficient and gallant commanding officer, Major J. E. Rylander, who was instantly killed at Cold Harbor or Gaine's Mill, on that date. "He was one of Georgia's most noble and worthy sons, and in his fall the battalion has sustained a most serious loss." Upon his death the command devolved upon Captain, now Major, James D. Frederick.

On the 22d and 23d of June, near Petersburg, the battalion suffered severely in battle, losing *eighty-one men in killed and wounded*, out of two hundred engaged. Upon the battle field of the 22d, the battalion was highly complimented by General Wright for its dashing gallantry.

The battalion was not engaged, with all the balance of Wright's Brigade (except the Second Georgia Battalion,) in the terrific battle of the 30th of July, it being on picket duty, three quarters of a mile in advance of the line of entrenchments, and probably about two miles from the scene of the explosion of Grant's mine, and the magnificent charge of Wright's Brigade.

That this little battalion deserves a great deal of credit, there can be no doubt, as its list of killed and wounded sufficiently attests, and it will be a matter of wonder to many of the readers of this work, that they ever managed to stand and be cut down as they were. The men were unused to fire, having been performing garrison duty almost from the time of its organization until the battle of the 14th of May, and could not be expected to bear themselves through the fight like the old veterans of Lee's army; but they did stand, did fight and proved the efficiency of the noble material of which it is composed.

They have reflected great credit upon their noble commander, who so "bravely fighting fell" on the 2d of June.

The present commander, Major Frederick, is a young man of great promise, who will, with his noble battalion, yet win a fame in his country's service.

GEORGIA VOLUNTEERS

———

The officers from whom I have collected the following material, are utterly unable to furnish me with the statistical matter I so much desire to head the history of each regiment with. The lamented Colonel Evans had promised me the very day before he met his fate, that he could and would furnish me with all statistical facts connected with his command; but I am of opinion that after his demise his papers were in great confusion, and the statistics were lost or mislaid.

Early in the spring of 1863, Colonel John W. Evans, of Bainbridge, Decatur County, received a commission from the Secretary of War to raise a regiment, to serve in Brigadier General Howell Cobb's command. Under that authority Colonel Evans proceeded to raise the different companies to compose said regiment, and on the 25th of May, consummated the organization at Quincy, Florida.

The regiment numbered forty-six officers and eight hundred and six privates, at the time it was mustered into service; embracing that class of troops comprehended in the third call of the President, viz: between the ages of eighteen and forty-five. Colonel Evans associated with himself Lieutenant Colonel James Barrow, and Major Walter H. Weems, as the field officers to command in said regiment.

A short time subsequent to its organization, the regiment was moved from Quincy, to Camp Leon, Florida, situated upon an open pine barren, six miles south of Tallahassee, for the purpose of defending the Gulf coast from Yankee raids. This service was in great part performed by detached companies as pickets, placed immediately along the coast. A point still further south was found to be more eligible for the location of a camp, and about the first of September the regiment was again moved to the place now known as Camp Randolph, fifteen miles south of Tallahassee, and six miles from St. Marks. At this camp there was great care displayed, upon the part of our commanding officers, in its general construction and military arrangement. Comfortable houses were built for the officers and men, wells were dug, and every convenience necessary for the comfort of the troops was attended to with scrupulous exactness. it may be doubted if there is a more complete regimental camp in the Confederate States, than was camp Randolph when the Sixty-fourth Georgia was ordered away It was at this camp that the regiment attained its maximum strength, to-wit: forty-two officers and eight hundred and twenty-nine privates. During the stay of the regiment at camp Randolph, the loss of the regiment by deaths, discharges and desertion, did not exceed one per cent. per month. On the 4th of January, 1864, the Sixty-fourth received orders to proceed to Savannah, Georgia, *via* Tallahassee, Monticello and Atlantic and Gulf railroad. On the 12th of January the regiment arrived and reported to Brigadier General Mercer, in Savannah, and was assigned to the command of General Colston, and went into camps under the guns of Fort Bartow, three miles from the city.

No incident transpired while at this camp worthy of record, unless it was the bloodless repulse of the enemy from Whitemarsh Island, who were at that time making some demonstrations along the coast of Georgia. From this camp the regiment proceeded by railroad to Quitman, upon the Atlantic and Gulf railroad; thence to Lake City, Florida.

When at this point information was obtained that the enemy were advancing from the direction of Jacksonville in large force, and the regiment was ordered to advance as far forward as Olustee station, on the Florida Central railroad. Here the command arrived on the evening of the 13th of February, with an efficient force, rank and file, of four hundred and eighty-six men. The first duty devolving upon this regiment, was to throw up breastworks, and prepare to the best of our ability to meet the heavy columns of the rapidly advancing foe. Other troops continued to arrive (among them the gallant brigade of Georgians, composed of the Sixth, Nineteenth, Twenty-third, Twenty-seventh and Twenty-eighth regiments, and commanded by General A. H. Colquitt,) for several days. All of whom, excepting Colquitt's Brigade, were placed under command of Colonel John W. Evans, with the very efficient Adjutant of the regiment, (J. A. Byrd) as Acting Adjutant General. On the morning of the 20th, the enemy had approached within eight miles of our entrenchments, when General Finnegan, who had now assumed command, ordered Colonel Evans to advance with the Sixty-fourth Georgia Regiment two miles to the front, and skirmish the enemy up to our main line. The order was promptly obeyed, and the regiment advanced with three hundred and thirty men, the balance being either sick or on detached duty. The line of battle had not been well formed, before our retiring cavalry gave indication of the near approach of the enemy.

Colonel Evans, Lieutenant Colonel Barrow, and Major Weems acted with the utmost coolness and bravery, each one exercising his influence upon and imparting courage to the troops, who had never been engaged before. Soon the shock fell, with frightful reality, upon the inexperienced ranks of the Sixty-fourth Georgia, and for a moment it required every effort on the part of the officers to keep their men in line. Indeed it was a fearful position to occupy, in the very face of fifteen thousand men who were pouring grape, canister and minnie balls into our lines like a tornado of hailstones. Our skirmishers in front were falling like leaves in autumn. After the first shock had subsided, and a few shots exchanged, the regiment was ordered to charge–because there was no order attended with less danger, which could have been given–and at the word, the regiment moved forward with a steadiness of purpose to conquer or die; and most gallantly for five hours was that resolution displayed upon that memorable battlefield.[*] Early in the action the noble and deeply to be lamented Lieutenant Colonel Barrow fell mortally wounded, with a ball through his generous heart. About the same time Major Weems received a severe wound in the leg, and was borne off the field.

Colonel Evans was left alone with his gallant Adjutant Byrd, to manoeuvre the regiment and inspire them with their own energy and hope. But it was not long before the Colonel received a wound which disabled him, and he too was borne off the field. The casualties in the regiment in this fight, were one hundred and ten in killed and wounded, or exactly one-third of the numbers carried into action. Many instances of individual courage occurred upon this field, but it is impossible to attempt to particularize, as there was scarcely a man on the field who did not bear himself as a hero. Captain C. S. Jenkins, assisted by the other captains and lieutenants, conducted the regiment through the most fearful periods of the fight,

---

[*] My informant must either have been mistaken regarding this affair, or omitted to mention the advance of the other troops, comprising the army of General Finnegan, as it was altogether improbable that the Sixty-fourth could have held the Yankee army at bay.

which of necessity became more desperate the nearer we approached the enemy's batteries, and as they were successively charged. Our trophies were numerous, but cannot be enumerated owing to want of space.

After caring for the wounded and burying the dead, the regiment was ordered forward in pursuit of the retreating enemy. This movement was performed as far as Camp Milton, ten miles in front of Jacksonville, the headquarters of the Yankee army in Florida. At this camp the regiment was stationed until about the 24th of April, throwing up breastworks, &c. The regiment numbered at this time thirty-eight officers and six hundred and forty privates, of these there were only two hundred and ninety-seven reported for duty. On the 24th of April the regiment received orders to proceed to South Florida, under command of Captain C. S. Jenkins, who had been in command since the loss of the field officers at Ocean Pond.

The regiment moved by railroad as far as Gainesville, Florida, in obedience to orders. Upon arriving at that point, Captain Jenkins ordered forward two companies as far as Clay Landing, to protect property, and defend that section against Yankee aggressions. These two companies, commanded by Captains Brown and Thomas, while on duty there, engaged the enemy and succeeded in repulsing them with some loss to the latter.

At this time Captain Jenkins received orders to report for duty at Richmond, Virginia, with the Sixty-fourth Georgia. In performing this journey, the regiment had to march from Madison to Quitman, Georgia, a distance of twenty-four miles, and which was the only marching between our point of departure and destination, (Petersburg, Virginia.)

On the 14th of May the regiment arrived at Petersburg, and was immediately placed by General Beauregard in the rifle pits along Swift Creek, which constituted a part of the defenses of the city of Petersburg. During this time the Sixty-fourth Georgia was in General Wise's Brigade, but the regiment was soon transferred across the Appomattox and placed in General Johnson's old Tennessee brigade, which occupied the left centre of the line of entrenchments, by order of General Beauregard. At this time the regiment was divided, four companies being retained for detached service on the north side of the river, and consequently but six companies participated in the battles of the 16th and 17th of June.

On the evening of the 16 of June, two brigades of the enemy charged the line occupied by the six companies of the Sixty-fourth Georgia, then under command of Captain Pritchett. It required all the nerve and energy of both officers and men to resist the impetuous assaults made upon our lines by the infuriated Yankees. Here again was displayed great courage and indomitable resolution, and every soldier steeled himself with an armor of invulnerable determination, which was soon to cause the foe to bite the sacred dust upon which his polluted feet had dared to make an impress. Well indeed was the task performed; as the enemy would advance and recede from our lines, like the ocean wave when maddened into fury by the howling blast, under the galling fire poured into them from the gallant Sixty-fourth, they went down by scores upon the gory field, rolling in their accursed life current which deeply dyed the soil of the Old Dominion, as it gushed from the wounds made by the leaden messengers of death, sped from the muzzles of the well directed muskets of the Sixty-fourth. The ordeal was too severe for their endurance, and the drama closed by the surrender of more than four hundred of the vandals, who found that it would be death to retreat. Captain Pritchett had the honor of commanding the regiment during this engagement, and is entitled to a due share of the credit which may attach to the capture.

Especial mention may be made of Captain Craven, Lieutenant T. J. Bartlett and Lieutenant A. M. Mound, as having particularly distinguished themselves in this engagement. Their remains now repose in honorable graves beneath the gory soil of the Old Dominion, upon whose breast, and for whose protection against the fierce foes of Southern independence, they poured out their hearts best blood as a libation to her glory. On the 17th the attack of the enemy was renewed upon our left with increased vigor, and so terrible were their assaults upon that part of our lines, that the brigade occupying that portion of the lines were forced to abandon their position in the trenches, thereby leaving the Sixty-fourth uncovered, and exposed to a most severe and destructive enfilading fire, which laid many of our brave boys low. This position of affairs, of course, rendered that part of the line occupied by the Sixty-fourth untenable, and that regiment, for the first time, was compelled to retire beyond the range of the enemy's guns. In this action Adjutant Byrd again exerted his utmost energies in rallying the troops and leading them into the abandoned trenches.

In the two engagements the loss of the Sixty-fourth in killed, wounded and missing, amounted to forty-five men.

On the 30th of July the sun rose upon another day which was to witness a deadly conflict, a desperate battle, and a glorious, decisive victory for the Confederacy.

The regiment at this time had combined all its companies, and numbered six hundred and thirty men rank and file; its efficient strength was three hundred and eighty-eight men, and with that number it entered into the desperate strife, which took place after the explosion of Grant's mine in our works. Immediately upon the explosion, and before the smoke had cleared away, the Yankees and negroes rushed into our line by thousands, and it became apparent that the only manner of dislodging them was by charging.

Wright's Brigade, of which the Sixty-fourth Georgia constituted a part, was drawn up in battle array, and received orders to charge. The order was promptly obeyed, and the Sixty-fourth, still under command of Captain Pritchett, acted its part in that deadly conflict with great gallantry, and a considerable degree of desperation, but the emergency demanded the most desperate remedies, and most faithfully did the Sixty-fourth administer them. The conflict was close and deadly; a hand to hand fight ensued and the hundreds of dead, and the thousands of the wounded hessians, attest the severity of the battle. But alas for poor humanity! There is no picture, however beautiful, but what has some spot to mar its symmetry, and in a degree detracts from its beauty. There is no joy on earth, of any duration, unalloyed with grief, and it seems that the very ground upon which the altar of liberty is to be erected, must first be sprinkled with the heart's blood of its devotees, or there can be no permanence to its superstructure. The picture of the thousands of dead and dying Yankees, the joy of our brave Georgia boys, made known to the world by their bugle shout of victory, had its reverse. The same earth that drank the life blood of our enemies, was also crimsoned with the same current, emanating from the noble hearts of many of the sons of our mother Georgia. With an unflinching determination to whip the fight, they rushed upon the guns of the enemy, and many of them

"Fiercely fighting fell."

Among the killed was Colonel Evans, who was not in command (not having resumed it, as he was one or two days behind his time in returning from home on furlough, and the rules of service require that no officer shall take his command until so permitted by General Lee,) being merely a volunteer. Seeing the line stagger under the withering fire poured into our ranks, he sprang upon the breastworks, and waving his hat over his head shouted, in tones which rang distinctly over the tumult of battle: "Remember, boys, you are Georgians," and at that moment received the shot through his generous, noble heart, which almost instantly terminated the mortal existence of as gallant and amiable a man as ever lived or died. The Sixty-fourth in this action lost heavily. Nine (9) officers were killed dead on the field, and twenty-five (25) privates and non commissioned officers, and fifty-four (54) were wounded, a large number mortally.[*]

This was the last action in which the Sixty-fourth Georgia participated, up to the time the above report was made out, (about the 10th of August.)

Major Weems will no doubt receive the appointment of colonel of the regiment, since the deaths of Colonel Evans and Lieutenant Colonel Barrow.

I am requested to publish, in connection with the above, a short article laudatory of the Assistant Quartermaster of the Sixty-fourth, but must decline to do so, as it would be decidedly unjust, in a work on and dedicated to the "Heroes and Martyrs of Georgia," to publish an article complimentary to one, (who is no doubt deserving all the encomiums which could be bestowed upon him, but who occupies a situation remote from danger,) in preference to those who *are* the "Heroes and Martyrs," but whose names I could not obtain, owing to the fact that all of the men acted as heroes, and to make distinctions would be insidious.

---

[*] The weather being intensely hot, and nearly every man being severely wounded, they died by scores. I am of opinion that seven-tenths of the wounded died.

PHILLIPS' LEGION

GEORGIA VOLUNTEERS

(CAVALRY)

———

The substance of the material composing the following pages was written upon the 29th of April of this year, but owing to the inefficiency of the Post Office Department, has just reached me (September 6th). I have tried several times, both by letter and personally, to communicate with the Legion, (cavalry) but have failed in every instance. I am satisfied that as many incidents of real importance have occurred in this command, since the 29th of April, as had occurred previously, and if it is possible I will obtain these incidents and give them a place in the second volume of this work.

Phillips' Legion, as originally organized by the Governor of Georgia, was composed of infantry and cavalry, and was commanded by Colonel William Phillips, of Cobb County. Seaborn Jones, Jr., of Polk County, was Lieutenant Colonel; John B. Wilcoxson, of Coweta County, Major; and James H. Lawrence, of Floyd County, Adjutant. The Legion was mustered into service on the 11th day of June, 1861, and consisted of ten companies. The Legion was prepared for active service in the field by drill and strict discipline, at Camp McDonald, in Cobb County, Georgia. From this place it was ordered to Lynchburg, Virginia. From Lynchburg it went to North Western Virginia, and served under General John B. Floyd, in one of the most severe campaigns of the war.

The winter of 1861, for its unusual severity, and the many and severe hardships to which this command was necessarily exposed, the campaign of Cotton Hill and Sewell Mountain will never fade from the memories of those who had the ill fortune to participate in their severities. The Legion being very much reduced was ordered to the coast of South Carolina, to which place it went in January, 1862. While here it composed a portion of the brigade of Brigadier General T. F. Drayton. During the stay of the Legion upon the coast of South

Carolina, no incident worthy of record occurred, except the change in field officers.

Lieutenant Colonel Seaborn Jones, Jr., and Major John B. Wilcoxson resigned. Captain William W. Rich, of Cass County, was in July, 1862, promoted to the position of Lieutenant Colonel, and assigned to the command of the cavalry companies of the Legion, who having received an accession to their strength of two companies, which augmented their number to six companies, were entitled to a Lieutenant Colonel and Major. Captain William B. C. Puckett, of Cherokee County, was in September, 1862, promoted Major. In July, 1862, the brigade of General Drayton received orders to proceed to Virginia and report to General Robert E. Lee for duty.

From that time until the present, the infantry and cavalry have been separated, and a subsequent order from the Secretary of War, created them separate and distinct organizations, so far as each other are concerned.* The Battalion under the command of Major Puckett, arrived at Shepherdstown in time to witness and participate in, to a limited degree, the world renowned battle of Sharpsburg. About the 20th day of September, 1862, the Battalion, still under command of Major Puckett, in compliance with orders, reported to Brigadier General Wade Hampton for duty, with whose command they have ever since served.

During the winters of 1862 and '63, the Battalion performed a great deal of hard duty, such as picketing, scouting and making raids. During those seasons the Battalion participated in a great many skirmishes, took many prisoners, weapons of war of all kinds, many head of horses, and in fact plundered the Yankees pretty generally. Passing over all the time intervening between the winter of 1862 and '63, the history of the Battalion is brought down to the month of June, 1863.

While the brigade was doing picket duty on the Rappahannock, and encamped in the vicinity of Culpepper Court House, Colonel Rich received orders from General Stewart to proceed at once to the vicinity of Fredericksburg and relieve the Fourth Virginia, then on duty there; which, upon their departure, left this Battalion the only cavalry in that neighborhood. At this time both the Yankee and Confederate armies were moving to Northern Virginia, and finally crossed the Potomac into Pennsylvania. This Battalion was left at Fredericksburg. Soon after the Battalion was ordered to rejoin Hampton's Brigade, which was in Loudon County,

---

* From this point only the Cavalry Battalion will be mentioned.

near Rectors Cross Roads. On the morning of the 21st of June, 1863, the command left Warrenton Springs, Fawquier County, passed through the village of Warrenton and were wending their way quietly along, until they arrived at a little place known as New Baltimore, where we were suddenly brought into pretty close contact with a squadron of the Eighth Pennsylvania cavalry. Colonel Rich ordered the second and third companies of the Legion Battalion to halt, and the first to charge, leading the column himself. The Yankees soon found that a desperate charge of a Georgia squadron was no trifling matter, and decided that the "signs of the times" were getting pretty warm, and all but one turned and fled for dear life. The Georgia troopers followed them about five miles at full speed, and succeeded in capturing twenty-three horses without losing a man. But one man in the Battalion was hurt, and that was Adjutant Wofford, who was struck on the breast with a pistol by the only Yankee that dared to face the column. He was a brave fellow, for after emptying his last round without effect, and receiving a severe cut on the head from the Adjutant's sabre, he used his pistol as a missile as the only remaining available weapon of defense. This was considered quite a brilliant little affair, and Lieutenant Colonel Rich was highly complimented by Brigadier General Hampton for his success. Upon rejoining the brigade each regiment gave three hearty, rousing cheers for the Phillips' Legion.

The Battalion participated in all the fights in which Hampton's Brigade was engaged in Pennsylvania, Maryland and Virginia, from that time until the present. The Battalion lost two officers killed during the campaign: Lieutenant E. M. Story, of Coweta, on the 9th of July, near Funkstown, Maryland, and Captain John F. Milhollin, of Cass, on the 8th of November, 1863, than whom no braver men have ever fallen in defense of their country's rights. About one hundred men were killed, wounded and taken prisoners during this campaign. The present strength of the Battalion is six hundred and forty-four men. The following is a list of the field officers, also company commanders, etc.:

W. W. Rich, *Lieutenant Colonel.*
W. B. C. Puckett, *Major.*
William E. Jones, *Chaplain.*
Calhoun Sams, *Surgeon.*
John W. Wofford, *Adjutant.*

Captains:–James H. Nichols, Thomas G. Wilkes, Eli C. Hardin, R. L. Y. Long, A. F. Hunter and W. W. Thomas.

ELEVENTH BATTALION

GEORGIA VOLUNTEERS

(CUTT'S ARTILLERY)

———

STATISTICAL REPORT TO APRIL 24TH, 1864.

No. of men killed in action, ...	28
" " " died of wounds and sickness, . . .	104
Total loss by death, ...	132
Discharged, ...	76
Deserted, ...	6
Transferred, ...	43
Missing and not heard from, ...	8
Total real loss, ...	265
Wounded in action, ...	154
Real and temporary loss, ...	419
Original strength Company A, ...	180
Recruits,*	376
Total strength, ...	556

Company A, upon which the Battalion known (and widely known,) as the Cutts' Battalion, was organized and formed in Sumter County, Georgia, by Captain A. S. Cutts, who, with his command left Americus, Georgia, on the 6th day of July, 1861, for Richmond, Virginia. This company was mustered into the service of the Confederate States on the 15th of July, and ordered to report to Manassas on the 24th of the same month. In the August following the company was equipped with six guns. The original number of men enlisted was one hundred and fifty, but in the fall of 1861 was

---

* I presume from the large number of recruits that my informant, Sergeant Major J. D. Harris, alludes to the companies which were added to company A, and which formed the battalion.

increased to one hundred and eighty men, and two more guns were added, making an eight gun battery of seven 6-pounders, and one 12-pound howitzer.

On the 20th of December the company was ordered to report to General Stuart with four guns, and it met the enemy at Dranesville in overwhelming force. We took position in a narrow country road walled in by a dense pine grove. The road was so narrow and the forest so thick, that there was no room to work but three guns. The enemy opened upon our little battery with 12-pounders from three different points at once, which could barely be discerned by the smoke from their pieces through the pines. The sharpshooters of the enemy poured a continuous and galling fire into this battery.

In one hour we suffered a loss of one caisson blown up, another demolished, a limber shot down, twenty horses killed, six men killed and fifteen wounded, out of forty cannoniers and drivers at the guns. In this fearful encounter, Captain Cutts rendered himself particularly conspicuous for desperate energy and cool, self-possessed, calculating courage. Lieutenant L. E. Sprivey (acting number five,) Privates Doolittle, Green and Lingo, and Sergeants Randall and Fletcher deserve special mention for their gallant conduct. Private J. L. Price at this place displayed that coolness and intrepidity which has marked his conduct ever since upon every battle field in which his company has been engaged; his name deserves to figure in the list of Georgia's heroes. Many others of the command behaved very handsomely.

In the spring of 1862, Captain Cutts was authorized to augment his command from a company to a battalion. Three more companies were recruited by him in Sumter County, Georgia, and Company A, of the Ninth Regiment of Georgia volunteers, having been detached from that regiment as an artillery company, was assigned to this battalion, thus making five companies in all. On account of much sickness and many deaths and discharges, one of the three new companies was disorganized and amalgamated into the remaining two new companies, thus reducing the Battalion to four companies. Captain Cutts was elected Major and soon afterwards promoted to the rank of Lieutenant Colonel. The battles in which we have participated are as follows:

Company A, at Drainesville in December, 1861; Company B, at Fredericksburg on the 2d day of May, 1863; Company C, at Richmond July, 1862, Warrenton Springs November, 1862, Washington, North Carolina, April, 1863, and Suffolk during the same month.

The whole Battalion was engaged in the night attack on McClellan's fleet and camp, on James river in July, 1862; also at Boonsboro, Sharpsburg and Fredericksburg, 1862, and at Gettysburg, 1863. After the battle of Sharpsburg one of the companies were broken up and the men distributed among the present three companies composing the Battalion; Company A, (original company) and B, from the county of Sumter, and Company C, from Wilkes County, Georgia. The present field officers are Lieutenant Colonel Cutts and Major John Lane. Colonel Cutts served for three years in the regular army of the United States, and two years in Mexico, during the war with that country in Steptoe's famous battery. From the experience thus acquired as well as from great natural fitness for command, he is a most excellent officer, and esteemed one of the best for artillery in the service. Promotion in this branch of service is of low grade and comes slowly, especially to any but Virginians, and our commander's rank does not fairly indicate either his merits or past services. As pertinent to this idea, Cutts' Battalion and the Jeff Davis Battery (another Georgia company) were all the artillery at the battle of Boonsboro on the Confederate side, and without support, kept back heavy masses of Yankee infantry during the entire day. In the official report of General D. H. Hill, the commanding General, they are not even mentioned.

Major John Lane is a son of General Joseph Lane, of Oregon, and a good officer. He is an under graduate of West Point, and warmly devoted to the cause of Southern Independence.

The small losses which this Battalion has sustained in battle, are mainly owing to the judicious manner in which the batteries have been posted by the field officers, and the skill and address with which the guns have been worked. All the batteries in this battalion are six gun batteries.

BATTALION RECORDS

FROM JANUARY 1ST, 1864, TO AUGUST, 1864.

On the 27th of February, Lieutenant Colonel Cutts was promoted to the rank of Colonel, and was, on the 5th of June, assigned to the command of a division of artillery, composed of his own and Lieutenant Colonel Richardson's Battalions. Major John Lane was assigned to the command of Cutts' Battalion. On the 4th of

May, this battalion, then temporarily attached to Anderson's Division, guarding the fords of the upper Rapidan, left winter quarters and proceeded to the Wilderness. In the battles which took place during the next two days at this point, the ground being impracticable for artillery, only a few guns were put into position, which few however, did effectual service in aiding to drive back some heavy columns of the enemy.

Arriving at Spottsylvania Court House on the 9th of May, the Battalion took position on the main road leading through this place to Richmond, and proceeded to fortify the point. Soon afterwards a column of the enemy approaching, a brisk fire was opened upon their ranks, when they retired with speed. For several days nothing transpired save a few artillery duels between the opposing guns, as no assault was made upon this portion of the line.

Arriving at Hanover Junction on the 23d of May, the Battalion went into position on the south bank of the North Anna river, between two fords on this stream, to resist the crossing of the enemy, and were almost immediately engaged in repelling his advance upon the infantry guard at the lower bridge. His guard being driven back,, the enemy next day commenced crossing in heavy force, under a vigorous and almost incessant fire from the guns, this Battalion, under command of Major Lane, Colonel Cutts being informally in charge of two battalions. So accurate and damaging was this fire that the Federal commanders resorted to the expedient of crossing only a few of their troops at a time, and these in straggling squads, while a long line of their artillery attempted to silence our guns. Several of the cannoniers were seriously wounded, some by the bursting of a 20-pounder parrot; but their comrades remained unshaken at their posts, although the enemy used *mortars* for the first time in the field, since the commencement of the war, in addition to a heavy direct fire. Nearly the whole artillery fighting in General Lee's army, while on these lines fell to the lot of Lane's Battalion.

General Grant continuing to move by the left flank the Battalion was ordered to —— Creek, where after some firing, and a few days on the lines, it took up the line of march for Cold Harbor, and there went into position on Turkey Ridge on 3d of June. After several days of more or less artillery dueling, it moved to the Chesterfield Heights on the north bank of the Appomattox, near Petersburg, and proceeded to fortify the position known as the Archer House. An enfilading fire was here obtained upon the enemy's line to the south, and fifteen guns, mostly rifles, from the battalions of the Third Corps were concentrated at this point under command of Major Lane, to check the enemy's fire from batteries one and five upon Petersburg, and two 30-pounder parrots added to his own battalion. To oppose this array of strength, the enemy brought into commanding positions on the opposite side of the river twenty odd guns, mostly 20 and 30-pound parrots, three eight inch mortars, and one thirteen inch. For five weeks Major Lane with inferior guns, and far inferior ammunition, fought the enemy more or less every day or night, with unyielding tenacity. Guns were disabled, works knocked down, many of the best and bravest men and officers killed and wounded; but new guns were mounted, the works rebuilt, and as often as the enemy's guns on that front sent a shot into the city, the iron watchdogs on Archer's Hill belched forth their thunders in its defense, forcing the vandals to turn from the shelling of women and children to defend himself. The Petersburg Press was loud in its praise of "our strong batteries on the Chesterfield side." Finally after in vain attempting to silence our guns, a sort of tacit truce prevailed. Whenever the enemy attempted to shell the town, a few shots from the Archer's House would produce perfect silence; the enemy ceasing their fire to prevent our guns from enfilading their infantry line. Under this arrangement the Federal batteries on our front became comparatively useless and were moved further to their left. Subsequently Major Lane with all the guns of his Battalion, except the two 30-pounders were ordered to the more immediate Petersburg front, and now holds position on the Jerusalem Plank road and other points to the westward.

THOMAS' BRIGADE

GEORGIA VOLUNTEERS

This Brigade was formed about the 15th of June, 1862, and was composed of the following named regiment:–

Fourteenth Georgia Regiment, Colonel Felix M. Price.
Thirty-fifth Georgia Regiment, Colonel Edward L. Thomas.
Forty-fifth Georgia Regiment, Colonel Thomas Hardeman, Jr.
Forty-ninth Georgia Regiment, Colonel A. J. Lane.

It was assigned to the Division of Major General A. P. Hill. The first commander of the brigade was Brigadier General Joseph R. Anderson of Virginia. Under the command of General Anderson, the brigade participated in the battles of Mechanicsville, fought June 26th; Gaines' Mill, June 27th; and Fraser's Farm, June 30th, 1862. Its effective strength when it crossed the Chickahominy on the afternoon of June 26th, was about seventeen hundred and fifty men. In the series of bloody battles which delivered the Southern capital from siege, this brigade lost five hundred and sixty-three men in killed and wounded.

About the 20th of July Brigadier General Anderson resigned, and the command of the brigade devolved upon Colonel Edward L. Thomas, who had commanded the Thirty-fifth Georgia Regiment with great success and gallantry in the above mentioned battles, and also the battle of Seven Pines. General A. P. Hill's Division being assigned to the command of General T. J. Jackson on July 31st, 1862, this brigade left the camp it had occupied since the battles around Richmond, and went to Gordonsville, where General Jackson's forces had collected. The brigade remained at Gordonsville until the 7th of August, when it moved with the rest of General Jackson's forces, by way of Orange Court House. On the 9th day of August, after a long and very hot march, General Jackson's command encountered the enemy under Major General Pope, near Cedar Run in Culpepper, where he utterly defeated them, driving them several miles from the field of battle. Thomas' Brigade behaved with distinguishing gallantry in this battle, checking the advance of the enemy on the extreme right of General Jackson's command, and holding them in check for some time, until after a long, obstinate and bloody fight, the order was given by General Jackson for a general charge, when the brigade advanced with the utmost bravery and enthusiasm, driving the enemy in utter rout before them. The loss of the brigade in this battle, known as the battle of Cedar Run, was about one hundred and fifty men in killed and wounded. Among the killed was Lieutenant Colonel S. M. Manning of the Forty-ninth Georgia Regiment, one of the best and bravest officers in the brigade.

For some time after this battle, Thomas' Brigade, with the rest of General Jackson's Corps, was encamped on Crenshaw's farm in Orange County, leaving which about the 23d of August, it proceeded under General Jackson on that celebrated flanking march, which by its successful accomplishment, placed the corps of the immortal Stonewall in the rear of Pope's Army. The astonishing boldness of this movement, the remarkable success and secrecy of its execution, the daring and obstinate bravery with which Jackson's Corps alone and unsupported, confronted and beat off Pope's Army on the 28th and 29th of August, are among the wonders of this war. No man except the hero who commanded that corps, could have kept men firm under circumstances so extraordinary. Thomas' Brigade was in reserve on the 28th of August. On the 29th it charged upon and routed with considerable slaughter, a force of the enemy on the Manassas Gap railroad, which position after having gained, the brigade held during the day. After a long and bloody fight of nine hours' duration, during which repeated charges of the enemy were repulsed, the brigade was driven from its position by an overwhelming force of the enemy; but uniting with Pender's North Carolina Brigade, with their assistance the enemy was finally driven back.

On the evening of August 29th the corps of Lieutenant General Longstreet arrived. The long agony of Jackson's Corps was now past, for five brave divisions had come to their assistance, and with their arrival, renewed confidence was instilled into the soldiers of Jackson, who, though by no means intimidated by the immense odds against which they were contending, were perfectly confident that with the heroes of Longstreet, they could hurl from their front the legions of Abolitionism. The next morning the conflict was renewed and raged desperately deadly. Pope's Army had been largely reinforced by the remains of McClellan's Peninsula Army. On that day, August 30th, the classic plains of Manassas were the scene of a long and bloody battle, and a most disastrous defeat on the part of the enemy, terminating in their utter rout. Thomas' Brigade fought on that day, and was among the foremost in the pursuit of the enemy. The brigade subsequently took part in the action near Chantilly on the 1st day of September, in which the enemy were again defeated and again routed.

General Lee's Army invading Maryland in 1862, Thomas' Brigade, with the rest of General A. P. Hill's Division, crossed the Potomac river near Leesburg on the 5th of September, and reached Frederick City two days thereafter. After a few days of rest the march was resumed, and recrossing the Potomac at Williamsport, reached Harper's Ferry *via* Martinsburg, on the 14th of September, and assisted in the capture of that place, together with the entire Federal force, numbering eleven thousand men. The brigade being ordered to remain at Harper's Ferry, was not present at the battle of Sharpsburg; it took part, however, in the subsequent affair near Shepherdstown. A force of the enemy having crossed the Potomac, Major General A. P. Hill turned upon them with Thomas', Gregg's and Pender's Brigades of his gallant and world renowned Light Division, and drove them in utter rout back across the river. For some time after this the army lay quiet, near Bunker Hill in the Valley of Virginia.

While here Colonel Felix M. Price having resigned, Lieutenant Colonel Robert W. Folsom was promoted to the Colonelcy of the Fourteenth Georgia Regiment. Colonel Thomas Hardeman having resigned, Lieutenant Colonel Thomas J. Simmons was promoted to the Colonelcy of the Forty-fifth Georgia Regiment. Colonel A. J. Lane having resigned, and Lieutenant Colonel S. M. Manning being killed, Major Jonathan Rivers was promoted to the Colonelcy of the Forty-ninth Georgia Regiment.

While in the Valley Colonel Edward L. Thomas was promoted to Brigadier General, to which position he has been recommended by Major General A. P. Hill immediately after the battles around Richmond, but the commission was not conferred upon him until the 1st of November, 1862, after he had repeatedly earned his wreath while commanding the brigade in several bloody battles.

About the 10th of November, 1862, the brigade left the Valley of Virginia, and crossing the Blue Ridge Mountains at Milom Gap, marched by way of Orange Court House to Fredericksburg. It remained encamped near that place until the 11th of December, when, General Burnsides having crossed the Rappahannock river with the Federal Army, the brigade took position near Hamilton's Crossing. It remained quiet, being in the second line, until December 13th, when the grand attack of the enemy took place. The troops in its front having been compelled by a strong column of the enemy to give back, Thomas' Brigade by a well directed and energetic charge, in turn drove back and utterly routed the Federals in its front. The brigade in this movement lost heavily. It remained in the front line and was not again engaged until relieved. The next day the Federal Army, badly beaten and demoralized, had recrossed the Rappahannock.

On the 30th day of April, 1863, the enemy having again crossed the river Rappahannock in front of Hamilton's Crossing, this brigade left its camp and marched to that point. On the 1st of May it proceeded towards Chancellorsville. On the 2d it moved with the rest of Jackson's Corps on that celebrated flank movement, by which the corps of the immortal Stonewall, making a detour of fourteen miles, gained the extreme right of the enemy's position, and surprised and routed two corps of them with great slaughter. Night put a stop to the rout of the enemy. Thomas' Brigade was placed in position during the night, on the extreme left of the front line. About daylight on the 3d of May, the order came to advance and attack the enemy at once. Without a moment's hesitation the brigade advanced, driving a line of the enemy's skirmishers before it, until having advanced about two hundred and fifty yards, the enemy were found in breastworks with an abatis in front, of trees which they had felled during the night. At once a charge was ordered by General Thomas, and without faltering an instant the brigade with a cheer, such as only Southern boys can give, rushed forward through a storm of balls, through the abatis and over the breastworks, driving the enemy's front line, supports, reserves and all, in a headlong rabble rout before them. This most gallant charge cost the brigade about two hundred men and officers killed and wounded; among them Lieutenant Colonel James M. Fielder of the Fourteenth Georgia, who was shot down in a few yards of the enemy's works, bravely leading on his men.

By this action and subsequent operations, the enemy having been driven back across the Rappahannock, the troops returned to their old camps near Fredericksburg. The glorious victory of

Chancellorsville cost the Confederate Army dear. Stonewall Jackson died soon after of wounds received in that battle,–leaving the country to mourn one of its purest and truest patriots, and the army to regret a leader under whose brilliant guidance it had so often marched to assured victory.

The Army of Northern Virginia being subsequently divided into three corps, Major General A. P. Hill was promoted to the rank of Lieutenant General, and Brigadier General W. D. Pender to Major General,–Thomas' Brigade then being in Pender's Division, A. P. Hill's Corps. About the middle of June the second invasion of the enemy's territory commenced. Thomas' Brigade marched by way of Culpepper Court House, Chester Gap, Berryville, Shepherdstown, Virginia, and Hagerstown, Maryland, into the State of Pennsylvania. The invasion ended with the battle of Gettysburg, in which Thomas' Brigade did not participate, except in very heavy skirmishing, and in being subjected to one of the most awful artillery fires ever witnessed. The loss of the brigade, however, amounted to about two hundred and fifty men, killed, wounded and prisoners.

After leaving Pennsylvania the brigade returned through the lower Valley, and across the Blue Ridge, to the vicinity of Orange Court House, where it remained in encampment until about the 9th of October, 1863, when the army again broke up camp and marched against the enemy encamped around Culpepper Court House. Thomas' Brigade was not engaged in the affair with the rear guard of the enemy at Bristow Station.

After destroying the railroad from Bull Run to the Rappahannock, our forces returned to their camps around Orange Court House, where they remained quiet until the latter part of the month of November, 1863, when the enemy under General Meade having crossed the Rapid Ann, General Lee advanced to meet him. Our line of battle was formed on the west side of Mine Run, across the plank road to Fredericksburg. General Meade seeing the disposition of our forces, returned across the Rapid Ann without coming to an engagement. The brigade of General Thomas remained in camp near Orange Court House until the 15th of December, when it was ordered to Staunton, Virginia, to repel a raid under General Averill. Subsequently it moved down the Valley as far as Middletown, to facilitate a movement of Major General Fitzhugh Lee's Cavalry Division across the North Mountain; after which in the month of January, 1864, with Rosser's Cavalry Brigade, both brigades being commanded by Major General J. A. Early, Thomas' Brigade left camp near Harrisonburg, Virginia, and crossing the North mountain, reached Moorfield, Hardy County, January 31st. The brigade on the ensuing day marched towards Petersburg, where the enemy had a force of three infantry regiments strongly entrenched; but they evacuated the post before the arrival of this brigade.

In the meantime General Rosser making a circuitous march, succeeded in surprising and capturing the enemy's supply train of one hundred and five (105) wagons, which with twelve hundred head of beef cattle, and six hundred sheep, were the fruits of the expedition.

The brigade returned to Orange Court House about the 5th of March, 1864, where it remained in quiet until the spring campaign of 1864 commenced.

By the resignation of Colonel S. T. Player and others, Captain J. T. Jordan was promoted about this time to Colonel of the Forty-ninth Georgia regiment.

During the winter of 1863 and '64, the Army of the Potomac was encamped around Culpepper Court House, Virginia, under the command of Major General Meade.

In the beginning of the month of May, the most arduous campaign of the war was inaugurated by the advance of the Yankee army from their winter quarters.

The Federal Government had been preparing for some months for another attempt to capture Richmond. A larger army was assembled than ever before, and placed under the command of Lieutenant General U. S. Grant, whose successes in the west gave his government the highest hopes of his abilities to capture the capitol of the Confederacy. The equipment of his army was in every respect complete.

A column of thirty thousand men under the command of Butler, the Beast, was to co-operate with General Grant, by way of the James river. General Grant's infantry force alone was computed at ninety-six thousand muskets; which with a numerous cavalry and artillery might well excite the hope in the hearts of the Northern people, that "the rebellion would now be crushed."

General Grant commenced crossing the Rapid Ann about the 3d of May. On the 4th General Lee left his camps around Orange Court House, and marched down the plank road and turnpike towards Fredericksburg. On the 5th of May he attacked the Federal forces with decided success in the "Wilderness."

On the evening of the 5th Thomas' Brigade was ordered into the action, with direction to proceed to the left of and form on McGowan's South Carolina Brigade, then engaged in a desperate fight with the enemy. While marching to execute this order, it was discovered that a strong column of the enemy had passed around the flank of the brigade and were in our rear. Under these circumstances, which were well calculated to test the courage and coolness of any troops in the most trying manner, General E. L. Thomas promptly faced the brigade to the rear, and attacked the enemy, repulsing them with heavy loss. This position was held until all fighting ceased. During the night Davis' Brigade, which had been in rear of Thomas' during the afternoon was retired, and Thomas' was left with the enemy in line in its front and rear, and on its right flank, totally unconnected with the balance of the division or any other supports. These unfavorable circumstances were reported by General Thomas to Major General Wilcox commanding the division, but produced no rectification of the line, and the brigade was ordered to remain in that position until relieved.

On the morning of the 6th, about day light, the brigade was attacked, at first only in front, this attack was successfully repulsed. While thus engaged another attack was made by the enemy upon our flank and rear in heavy force, while at the same time they were steadily closing the only avenue of escape left to the brigade. This state of affairs rendered it necessary to withdraw, which was done by the left flank in great confusion, together with the rest of the division. This very unfortunate affair cost this brigade many valuable officers and men, among them one of its best officers, Colonel Robert W. Folsom, of the Fourteenth Georgia regiment, whose zeal, energy and true patriotism, rendered him, though but a young man, a most distinguished soldier, and known as such throughout the army of Northern Virginia. The responsibility for this useless shedding of precious blood, does not rest upon any officer of Thomas' Brigade.

Leaving the gory field of the Wilderness, the brigade marched to Spottsylvania Court House. Here it was engaged on May 12th in repulsing the desperate effort of the enemy to break General Lee's centre.

The battle lasted from daylight in the morning until past midday, and was one of the bloodiest and hardest contested fields of the war. The enemy were finally repulsed with a slaughter so sickening that the heart heaves at the details. Thomas' Brigade acted gallantly and suffered severely. It drove the enemy out of and past a portion of our line, from which they had previously driven a portion of our forces. The brigade then retired to the recaptured portion of the line and held it.

Leaving Spottsylvania Court House about the 20th of May, the brigade arrived south of the North Anna river on the 21st, where for several days the army was in line of battle, but were not attacked by the enemy. From this position General Lee's army moved across the South Anna, constantly confronting the Federal army, and warding it off from Richmond, until Grant's left and General Lee's right rested upon the Chickahominy river, near the Grapevine bridge, and Cold Harbor. Here General Grant made a desperate effort to break our lines, but was repulsed with immense slaughter, while our loss was very small. Thomas' Brigade was not actively engaged in this affair, known as the battle of Cold Harbor. Failing so signally at this point, General Grant moved his army across the James river and appeared about the middle of June in front of the city of Petersburg, which city he has not as yet succeeded in capturing, having been repulsed with great loss in several desperate assaults.

At Mechanicsville, Gaines' Mill, Fraser's Farm, Cedar Run, Manassas No. 2, Chantilly, Harpers Ferry, Shepherdstown, Fredericksburg, Chancellorsville, Gettysburg, in the Wilderness, on the Ny, and the Appomattox, this brigade has proven its devotion to the great principle for which we have taken up arms.

Many a gallant brother in arms have we buried in Old Virginia's soil, many a disabled comrade has left our side, bearing on this body the marks of the terrible battle field. We are now few, but we are still undismayed. With an unshaken confidence in God, we stand ready now as heretofore to meet the foe.

BRIGADIER GENERAL AND STAFF, AUGUST 8TH, 1864.

Edward L. Thomas, *Brigadier General.*
Captain William Arnold, *Assistant Adjutant General.*
Captain W. J. Gorham, *Assistant Adjutant and Inspector General.*
Lieutenant E. L. Lewis, *Aid-de-Camp.*
Major R. T. Taylor, *Brigade Quartermaster.*
Major Lewis Ginter, *Brigade Commissary.*
Captain J. W. Moore, *Assistant Commissary.*
Lieutenant S. F. Tenny, *Brigade Ordnance Officer.*

REGIMENTAL COMMANDERS, AUGUST 8TH, 1864.

Fourteenth Georgia Regiment, Major W. L. Goldsmith.
Thirty-fifth Georgia Regiment, Lieutenant Colonel W. H.
        McCullohs.
Forty-fifth Georgia Regiment, Colonel T. J. Simmons.
Forty-Ninth Georgia Regiment, Colonel J. T. Jordan.

GEORGIA VOLUNTEERS

STATISTICAL RECORD.

STRENGTH OF REGIMENT.

Originally enlisted and recruited, ... 1160

LOSSES IN EACH ENGAGEMENT.

Place and Date.	Killed.	Wounded.
Seven Pines, May 31st, 1862, ...	11	52
Mechanicsville, June 26th, 1862, ...	4	26
Cold Harbor, June 27th, 1862, ...	4	20
Frazer's Farm, June 30th, 1862, ...	5	11
Malvern Hill, July 1st, 1862, ...	2	5
Cedar Run, August 9th, 1862, ...	16	39
Manassas, No. 2, August 29th and 30th, 1862, .	13	51
Ox Hill, September 1st, 1862, ...	3	5
Harper's Ferry, September 15th, 1862, ...		6
Shepherdstown, September 19th, 1862, ...	1	4
Fredericksburg, December 13th, 1862, ...	12	47
Chancellorsville, May 3d, 1863, ...	7	41
Gettysburg, Pennsylvania, July 1st, 2d and 3d, 1863,	14	58
Mine Run, November 27th, 1863, ...	1	
Wilderness, May 5th and 6th, 1864, ...	23	68
Spottsylvania Court House, May 12th, 1864, . .	4	18
Jericho Ford, May 23d, 1864, ...	2	11

Nances' Shop, June 23d, 1864, ...	2	1
Total casualties, ...	124	463
Number of men died of disease, . . .	289	
Number of men died of wounds, . . .	18	
Total deaths, ...	431	
Number of men discharged, ...	194	
Number of men transferred, ...	5	
Number of men deserted, ...	6	
Total real loss, ...	636	
Add number of men wounded, ...	463	
Total of all losses, ...	1099	

The Forty-ninth Regiment of Georgia Volunteers was organized under a call for volunteers, by Governor Joseph E. Brown, on the 4th day of March, 1862, and was composed of the following named companies, to which are appended the names of the officers:

Company A, Wilkinson County–Captain S. T. Player, Lieutenants James B. Duggan, J. Walker, J. R. F. Miller. Number of men enlisted, one hundred and thirty-six, (136) of whom four (4) were promoted; seventeen (17) killed in action, thirty (30) died of disease, thirteen (13) discharged and retired, and two (2) deserted.

Company B, Telfair County–Captain James Humphrey, Lieutenants James Y. Wilcox, William Hatton, L. L. Williams. Number of men enlisted one hundred and twelve, (112) of whom three (3) were promoted; twelve (12) killed in action, twenty-six (26) died of disease, and six (6) discharged and retired.

Company C, Washington County–Captain W. W. Carter, Lieutenants N. H. Clay, J. T. Jordan, M. Newman. Number of men enlisted eighty-one, (81) of whom five (5) were promoted; twelve (12) killed in action, twenty-two (22) died of disease, and thirteen (13) discharged or retired.

Company D, Taliaferro County–Captain William F. Holden, Lieutenants E. D. Rhodes, John A. Durham, L. M. Andrews. Number of men enlisted one hundred and five, (105) of whom four (4) were promoted; twenty (20) killed in action, twenty-one (21) died of disease, and eighteen (18) discharged and retired.

Company E, Wilcox County–Captain J. D. Fuller, Lieutenants D. S. McCall, P. Brown, R. D. Bowen. Number of men enlisted one hundred and seventeen, (117) of whom four (4) were promoted; eighteen (18) killed in action, forty-two (42) died of disease, and fourteen (14) discharged and retired.

Company F, Irwin County—Captain O. H. Cooke, Lieutenants R. W. Clements, R. Tucker, L. G. Young. Number of men enlisted one hundred and twenty-six, (126) of whom four (4) were promoted; six (6) killed in action, forty-two (42) died of disease and twenty-eight (28) discharged or retired.

Company G, Laurens County—Captain J. T. Chappell, Lieutenants J. A. Daniel, R. H. Duncan, C. C. Clark. Number of men enlisted one hundred and thirty, (130) of whom four (4) were promoted; fourteen (14) killed in action, thirty-four (34) died of disease, twenty (20) discharged and retired, and one (1) deserted. The deserter was not a native of Laurens County.

Company H, Washington County—Captain C. M. Jones, Lieutenants A. D. Jennigan, T. W. Newsome, L. M. Kinmon. Number of men enlisted eighty-nine, (89) of whom four (4) were promoted, seven (7) killed in action, twenty-eight (28) died of disease, twelve (12) discharged and retired, one (1) transferred, and two (2) deserted. The two deserters were assigned to this company from Echols county; they were not citizens of Washington county.

Company I, Hancock County—Captain A. J. Lane, Lieutenants J. J. Lawrence, L. L. Lamar, William Amos. Number of men enlisted, ninety-eight, (98), of whom six (6) were promoted; thirteen (13) killed in action, twelve (12) died of disease, nineteen (19) discharged and retired, two (2) transferred to non-commissioned staff, and one (1) deserted. The deserter was a native of Ireland.

Company K, Pulaski County—Captain S. M. Manning, Lieutenants W. H. Whitfield, John H. Pate, E. A. Smith. Number of men enlisted, one hundred and twenty-four, (124) of whom seven (7) were promoted; thirteen (13) killed in action, twenty-four (24) died of disease, and eighteen (18) discharged and retired.

The above named companies rendezvoused at Camp Davis, near Savannah, Georgia, and on the 22d day of March, 1862, completed the organization of the regiment by the election of the following field officers:—

Colonel:—Captain A. J. Lane, of Hancock County.
Lieutenant Colonel:—Captain S. M. Manning, of Pulaski County.
Major:—Private Jonathan Rivers, of Wilkinson County.

The following staff appointments were made by Colonel Lane, which were subsequently confirmed by the Secretary of War._

Thomas Latimer,–*Adjutant.*
J. M. Harris,–*Assistant Quartermaster.*
J. W. Moore,–*Assistant Commissary Subsistence.*
James J. Humphries,–*Surgeon.*
R. H. Pate,–*Assistant Surgeon.*
J. J. Hyman,–*Chaplain.*

Of the forty-six (46) officers above enumerated, six (6) were killed in action, five (5) died of disease, twenty-five (25) resigned, two (2) transferred, and two (2) cashiered. The remaining six (6) original officers are:–Lieutenant J. T. Jordan, (now Colonel), Lieutenant James B. Duggan, (now Major), Lieutenant M. Newman, (now Adjutant), Lieutenant L. M. Andrews, (now Captain), Lieutenant L. L. Williams, (now Captain), and Chaplain J. J. Hyman. All the other officers in the regiment at the present time, September 1st, 1864, have been elected and promoted by seniority since the organization.

The intervening time between the organization and the departure of the regiment for Goldsboro, North Carolina, on the 2d of April, 1862, was occupied in daily drills in the manual of arms and the school of the soldier. Upon its arrival at Goldsboro it was incorporated into the brigade of General Joseph R. Anderson of Virginia, who at that time had command at that point.

Diseases incident to camp life, such as measles and dysentery, became alarmingly prevalent in the regiment, detaining it in camp some three weeks longer than the other regiments of the brigade, who had received orders and left for Virginia about the 1st of May, 1862. After the departure of General Anderson, this regiment was assigned to the brigade of General William Walker, wherein it remained until the health of the men was sufficiently restored to enable them to proceed to Richmond. Accordingly on the 24th day of May, 1862, the regiment was transported to Virginia by railroad, with orders to report again to General Anderson; but upon the arrival of the Forty-ninth in Richmond, it was considered impracticable to join General Anderson's command, which was then stationed near Guinea's Station on the Fredericksburg railroad, and it was assigned temporarily to the brigade of General Pettigrew, under whose command it engaged in the battle of Seven Pines on the 31st of May, sustaining a loss of eleven killed and fifty-two wounded.

The Forty-ninth Georgia encountered the enemy with a coolness and determination, hardly to have been expected from troops who then went under fire for the first time. Yet such was their conduct on that occasion, as to elicit the remark of General Joseph E. Johnston, which was uttered in the hearing of several officers, "Those men move like veterans."

Under a galling fire of grape, canister and minnie balls, the regiment moved steadily on until ordered to retreat. General Pettigrew having been seriously wounded and fallen into the hands of the enemy, the regiment was, on the 3d of June, placed in a brigade of which General Pender of North Carolina, had just assumed command, under whom it remained a short time, when it was finally again joined to the brigade of General Anderson. Daily drills and picket duty on the defenses near the Mechanicsville turnpike, were the occupation of the regiment till the movement began on the 24th of June, which culminated in the "Seven Days' Battles around Richmond."

The brigade having been assigned to Major General A. P. Hill's Division, widely known as the Light Division, this regiment with the others of the brigade, crossed the Meadow bridge over the Chickahominy on the 26th of June, and was soon engaged in the Battle of Mechanicsville, sustaining a loss of four killed and twenty-six wounded. Colonel Lane who had ably commanded the regiment in the battle of Seven Pines and in this battle, was here so seriously wounded as to disable him for further field service. At the battle of Cold Harbor on the 27th of June, the regiment was again engaged, being gallantly led by Lieutenant Colonel Manning, in the several assaults against the enemy's strongly fortified positions, on which occasions it sustained a loss of four killed and twenty wounded. At the battle of Fraser's Farm on the 30th of June, in the absence of Lieutenant Colonel Manning, who was too weak from exhaustion to participate in it, Major Jonathan Rivers led the regiment, inspiring the men with an enthusiasm gleaned from his own enthusiastic and generous nature. The losses of the regiment in this engagement amounted to five killed and eleven wounded, and the capture of Major Rivers, who regardless of all danger, had gone ahead of the regiment on a reconnoissance. At the battle of Malvern Hill on the 1st of July, Lieutenant Colonel Manning, though feeble and almost exhausted, again led the regiment. The battle was nearly over when the Forty-ninth became engaged; but it nevertheless sustained a loss of two killed and five wounded. In this series of engagements the regiment fought with a coolness and bravery second to none in the service of the Confederate States, showing a determination to sacrifice their lives if necessary, in the achievement of our independence.

General Anderson having been wounded at the battle of Fraser's Farm, the command of the brigade, composed of the Fourteenth, Thirty-fifth, Forty-fifth and Forty-ninth Georgia Regiments, devolved upon Colonel Edward L. Thomas, of the Thirty-fifth. For gallantry in the battle of Cold Harbor, Private W. J. Williams of Company B, was promoted to the First Lieutenancy of that Company, that position having become vacant by the promotion of Lieutenant Wilcox to the captaincy. While the regiment was recuperating after the close of this campaign, a number of officers tendered their resignations, which in all cases were accepted. Among the number was Surgeon J. J. Humphries, which position was soon thereafter filled by the assignment of Surgeon J. J. Dement, formerly of the Twenty-seventh Alabama Regiment.

About the latter part of July, 1862, the war notes sounded once more, arousing the army for active preparations. On the 29th of that month the regiment received marching orders for, and on the 1st day of August arrived at Gordonsville. The Second Army Corps having at that time been organized, it was the good fortune of Hill's Light Division to be assigned to it. Already had the fame of that glorious chieftain, Stonewall Jackson, spread over two continents, and it was rightly esteemed by this regiment a glorious privilege to fight under his banners.

The stillness of the beautiful morning of the 9th of August, was rudely broken by the sharp rattle of musketry on the Rapid Ann. Soon the army was in motion, and at three o'clock, P.M. encountered the enemy on Slaughter Mountain, at Cedar Run. This regiment was assigned a position on a range of hills, from which a favorable view of the enemy's position was obtained and well did the Forty-ninth use the advantage thus obtained. An almost uninterrupted volley of musketry was poured into the enemy's ranks until the ammunition was exhausted. Eagerly did the men grasp the proffered cartouch boxes, which some of the officers took from the killed and wounded, nor did the regiment move from its position until darkness had ended the contest, although for nearly an hour it had stood with bayonets fixed, and not a single cartridge in their boxes. Early in the action, Lieutenant Colonel Manning, who had nobly led the men into the fight, fell seriously wounded from the effects of which he died on the 9th of September. Captain Wilcox of Company B, another gallant officer, here fell mortally wounded. The name and gallant deeds of these two officers, will ever live in the memories of their surviving comrades. The regiment lost in this engagement, sixteen killed and thirty-nine wounded. During the engagement the Colonel commanding the brigade found it necessary to strengthen the extreme right of the line; and for that purpose Captain John H. Pate of Company K, was detached with two companies to execute that movement, in which he acquitted himself gallantly. After the fall of Lieutenant Colonel Manning, in the absence of Major Rivers who was still a prisoner, the command of the regiment devolved upon Captain S. T. Player of Company A, who successfully conducted its operations until the close of the action.

The return of Major Rivers from Fort Warren on the 23d of August, (he having been exchanged) was hailed with lively satisfaction by the regiment. Assuming command once more, he gallantly led it into the second battle of Manassas, on the 29th and 30th of August, on which occasion, the regiment bore itself with its usual gallantry, participating in the ever memorable charge under the lead of General Pender, thereby aiding in the achievement of a glorious victory over the armies of the United States, at that time commanded by General Pope. In this battle the losses in the Forty-ninth amounted to thirteen killed, and fifty-one wounded.

While the regiment with the others of Thomas' Brigade were moving cautiously on the Fairfax turnpike, on the 1st of September, heavy skirmishing on the right discovered the presence of the enemy. Near Chantilly the regiment was deployed into a corn field, and were soon engaged in the battle of Ox Hill, during a severe storm of rain. The enemy kept up a furious shelling of our line, which continued until long after dark. The opposing forces became engaged in an almost hand to had fight at this point, during which Major General Kearney of the United States Army was killed by Sergeant McCrimmon, of Company B of this regiment, who succeeded in capturing his horse and accoutrements. The horse was subsequently sent to the family of General Kearney, by order of General Lee. In this engagement the loss was three killed and five wounded. Among the latter was Major Rivers, who was so severely wounded that amputation of the right foot became necessary, disabling him from further service in the field. Once more the command of the regiment devolved upon Captain Player, an officer of ripe age and extensive experience on several hard fought battle fields, who led it successfully through the engagement at Harper's Ferry on the 15th of September, and while there guarding the vast stores captured at that point. The loss sustained here was six men wounded; fortunately none were killed.

The army having recrossed the Potomac, the regiment was furiously shelled, and became engaged with the enemy at Shepherdstown, losing one killed and four wounded. At Bunker Hill and Berryville the regiment was encamped, doing picket duty at intervals on the Charlestown road, until the 22d of November, when the army commenced a retrograde movement in the direction of Fredericksburg. After an uninterrupted march of twelve days, having crossed the Blue Ridge at New Market, the regiment on the 2d day of December encamped five miles from Fredericksburg. While at Bunker Hill vacancies in the regiment were filled by promotion and election. The position of Lieutenant Colonel having become vacant by the death of Lieutenant Colonel Manning, Major Rivers was promoted to Lieutenant Colonel, and Captain Player to Major.

Under the command of the latter the regiment went into the battle of Fredericksburg on the 13th of December, where it fully sustained its former reputation for dash and gallantry, losing twelve killed and forty-seven wounded. With the battle of Fredericksburg ended the campaign of 1862.

On the 17th of December the Forty-ninth went into winter quarters near Guinea's Station, doing picket duty on the banks of the Rappahannock, and performing regular drills when in camp.

During the month of April, 1863, notes of preparation for the opening of the spring campaign began to sound once more. Baggage was sent to the rear and all the signs of the times indicated an early clash of arms. On no occasion had the health of the regiment been better, and the men in the full play of all their physical powers were ready and eager for the fray. A liberal system of furloughing had been instituted during the past winter, giving many soldiers the opportunity to visit home and its loved ones, and who, on returning, were nerved anew to fight for all that is dear to man.

Under these favorable auspices the battle Chancellorsville, on the 3d of May, 1863, was fought, where the well appointed, and so much boasted of "Grand Army of the Potomac," met with a most crushing, overwhelming defeat that had ever befallen the army of the Federal Government. In this engagement the regiment, under the command of Major Player, performed its assigned duties with a precision and gallantry unsurpassed by any former occasion. The charge on the enemy's works by this regiment on the morning of the 3d of May, was an achievement well calculated to elate the men with a just pride. The loss was seven killed and forty-one wounded.

Returning from this battle the regiment again encamped in a lovely oak grove, which it had so recently abandoned. Here again, as usual when in camp, the regiment passed through the usual routine of camp duties, such as drilling occasionally and performing picket duty on the banks of the Rappahannock, but on the whole enjoying comparative repose. On the 9th of June, 1863, a feint movement of the enemy upon Fredericksburg, drew the army once more from its retirement. This regiment with the others of Thomas' Brigade, occupied the trenches about one mile from Hamilton's Crossing until the 15th of June, when it set out on the march into the State of Pennsylvania, where the regiment participated in the battle of Gettysburg, on the 1st, 2d and 3d of July, losing fourteen killed and fifty-eight wounded.

On account of his ill health Major Player was not with the regiment in this action, which was commanded on the march by Captain C. M. Jones, of Company H, and in the battle by Captain O. H. Cooke, of Company F. The loss of Captain Jones, who was killed while leading a charge of the skirmishers of the brigade, which he commanded on the evening of the 2d of July, was deeply deplored by the entire regiment. He was a young but gallant officer, who had, by his bravery and affability, won the esteem of all whose privilege it was to associate with him. Here too Lieutenant Young, of Company F, a faithful and meritorious officer was killed while charging the enemy.

The resignation of Colonel Lane and Lieutenant Colonel Rivers having been accepted, it became necessary on the return of the regiment from Pennsylvania, to fill the vacancies that had occurred in it; whereupon the promotion of the following named officers, as well as the corresponding promotions in the line officers, were announced:

Major S. T. Player, as Colonel from June 9th, 1863.
Captain O. H. Cooke, as Lieutenant Colonel from July 28th, 1863.
Captain J. H. Pate, as Major from July 28th, 1863.

The regiment once more in camp, enjoyed repose until the 9th of October, when the army set out on the campaign, having for its object the driving of Meade's army into the entrenchments around the City of Washington–which movement was only partially successful–and ended in the occupation by the army of Northern Virginia of the country around Brandy Station, until the 9th of

November, when the regiment once more returned to camp near Orange Court House.

Colonel Player, Lieutenant Colonel Cooke, and Major Pate, having been elected to represent their fellow citizens and soldiers in the Legislative branch of the Councils of Georgia, and had left for that State, the regiment, under the command of Captain J. T. Jordan, of Company C, set out on the 27th of November on the campaign which terminated at Mine Run. The enemy having been confronted by General Lee's army for five days, did not venture to attack it, and recrossed the Rapidan. During the five days the weather was so intensely cold that it was found necessary to relieve the pickets and skirmishers every half hour, to prevent them from freezing on their posts. On this occasion the men bore their hardships with the fortitude which had always characterized them. The loss was one man killed.

On the 15th of December, while preparing winter quarters, this regiment with the balance of General Thomas' Brigade, were ordered to report to Major General Jubal A. Early, who with other forces that were assigned to him, set out upon a campaign into the Shenandoah Valley, having in the meantime made an unsuccessful attempt to intercept the raid of Averill, near Millboro.

While on this expedition the regiment aided in driving the enemy from his well fortified position near Moorfield, Hardy County, in spite of the inclemency of the weather which it bore with its wonted cheerfulness.

On the 6th of March, 1864, the regiment arrived at Orange Court House, and went into camps again, building chimneys to the tents, and making itself otherwise as comfortable as the nature of the situation would admit of.

A very liberal system of furloughing having again been inaugurated, many of the officers and men had the delightful privilege of visiting "those they loved so well."

Lieutenant Colonel Cooke and Major Pate having availed themselves of the privilege attached to their positions as Senator and Representative in the Legislature of Georgia, resigned their commissions. Colonel Player having failed to obtain a leave of absence, to attend an extra session of the Georgia General Assembly, felt it due to his constituents to tender his resignation as Colonel, which was accepted on the 24th of March, 1864. In consequence of these resignations, the following promotions were announced, as well as the corresponding promotions in the line:

Captain J. T. Jordan, Colonel, to date from 24th March, 1864.
Captain W. J. Williams, Lieutenant Colonel, to date from March 24th, 1864.
Captain John A. Durham, Major, to date from March 24th, 1864.

Under command of Colonel Jordan the regiment, with greatly diminished numbers, entered into its third year's campaign, which opened with the battle of the Wilderness, on the 5th and 6th of May, 1864, where against tremendous odds the regiment repulsed, with its usual stubbornness, the repeated assaults of the enemy. On the morning of the 6th, it had to vacate the position which had been assigned to it during the previous night, owing to the fact, that in the sudden onslaught of the enemy in such overwhelming force the regiment found itself almost entirely surrounded.*

Having extricated itself from this dangerous position, it soon rallied again on the Orange and Fredericksburg plank road, and formed on the other regiments of the brigade, who had been similarly assaulted, and who had received a similar repulse. In this engagement the regiment lost twenty-three killed and sixty-eight wounded.

The movement of the enemy by the left flank, and the corresponding movements of General Lee's army, are familiar to every reader of the events of the day. On the 12th of May, in the battle of Spottsylvania Court House, the regiment lost four killed and eighteen wounded, and at Jericho Ford, on the 23d, two killed and eleven wounded. Here Major Durham, while rallying a portion of the regiment which had unaccountably given way, fell mortally wounded. He was a gallant soldier, a faithful officer, he knew no fear on the field of battle. He died much lamented on the 11th of June. In the skirmish at Nance's Shop, June 23d, the regiment lost two killed and one wounded.

In the siege of Petersburg the regiment has occupied several positions upon its defensive lines. Captain James B. Duggan was promoted to Major to fill the vacancy occasioned by the death of Major Durham, on the 11th of June.

Since his promotion Colonel Jordan has acquitted himself creditably, and to the complete satisfaction of his superior officers,

---

* For more full particulars of this affair, see history of Thomas' Brigade in the preceding chapter.

and in such a manner as to acquire the respect and esteem of his subordinates. On all occasions, and with but few exceptions, both officers and men have vied with each other in the faithful performance of the duties assigned to them; nor did they shrink from or shirk these duties, however arduous or perilous they might have been.

While the loss of the gallant men of this regiment, who have given their lives in the cause of their country, is severely felt and long mourned, it is the unalterable determination of their surviving comrades never to relinquish the struggle until the flags of all nations lower in salute to the cross of the Confederacy, until our independence we have so bravely and nobly won is recognized, and our beloved country takes her place among the nations of the earth.

Among the many heroes whose names stand high on the roll of fame, from old Georgia, the gallant, daring, desperate deeds of courage of Lieutenant John B. Roberts, scout for Wilcox's Division, bears second rank to none, and he has gained for himself a name which will long be prominent in the Empire State of the South. He has frequently penetrated to the very heart of the Yankee camp, and returned in safety bearing information of the greatest value. He has taken prisoners in their lines and undergoing great personal risk, brought them triumphantly into camp. He has also seized videttes upon their posts and marched them into our lines. His courage is not the result of impulse, but of that cool and deliberate character which renders him a dangerous enemy.

Surgeon J. J. Dement and Chaplain J. J. Hyman have rendered services which deserve more than a passing notice, but I am unfortunately compelled to adhere to the rule laid down at the close of the history of the Sixty-fourth Georgia Regiment.

THIRTY-FIFTH REGIMENT

GEORGIA VOLUNTEERS

STATISTICAL RECORD.

STRENGTH OF REGIMENT.

Number of men originally enlisted, ... 740
"   "   recruited and conscribed, ... 535
        Total strength, ... 1275

LOSSES IN EACH ENGAGEMENT.

Place.	Killed.	Wounded.
Seven Pines, ...	23	50
Mechanicsville, ...	18	61
Other battles around Richmond, ...	3	13
Cedar Run, ...	9	17
Manassas No. 2, ...	18	55
Ox Hill, ...		1
Harper's Ferry, ...		4
Shepherdstown, ...		9
Fredericksburg, ...	14	41
Chancellorsville, ...	8	27
Gettysburg, ...	9	53
Mine Run, ...		2
Wilderness, ...	4	22
Spottsylvania, ...	10	37
Jericho Ford, ...	10	28

Hames' Shop, ...	2	6
Near Petersburg, ...	—	3
Total casualties, ...	128	429

Total loss of the regiment from deaths on the field of battle, and from wounds and disease, discharges, transfers and desertions six hundred and sixty (660).

The Thirty-fifth Georgia Regiment (Infantry) was composed of the following companies:

Company A, Captain W. J. Head, from Haralson County.

Company B, Captain J. M. White, from Newton County.

Company C, Captain D. B. Henry, from Campbell County.

Company D, Captain L. A. J. Williams, from Troup and Heard Counties.

Company E, Captain E. R. Whitley, from Campbell County.

Company F, Captain R. M. Rawlins, from Gwinnett County.

Company G, Captain W. S. Barrett, from Walton County.

Company H, Captain A. R. Richardson, from Gwinnett and Hall Counties.

Company I, Captain W. L. Groves, from Chattooga County.

Company K, Captain W. H. McCulloh, from Harris County.

It was organized in Richmond, Virginia, November 1st, 1861, with E. L. Thomas, Colonel; G. A. Bull, Lieutenant Colonel; B. W. Holt, Major; J. H. Ware, Company K, Adjutant; Dr. J. P. Hambleton, Surgeon; Dr. P. E. L. Jennings, Assistant Surgeon; Captain L. P. Thomas, Quartermaster; Captain V. L. Hopson, Commissary Subsistence; Rev. G. W. Yarborough, Chaplain. Numbering in the aggregate forty-eight (48) officers and six hundred and ninety-two (692) enlisted men.

Upon the completion of its organization, the regiment was assigned to the command of Brigadier General French, and stationed at Evans' Port, Virginia, and at that point remained supporting the river batteries, until early in March, 1862. It followed the Army of the Potomac to the line of the Rappahannock, and was stationed near

Fredericksburg, Virginia. Here Brigadier General J. J. Pettigrew was assigned to the command of the brigade to which this regiment was attached.

The Thirty-fifth participated in the remove to the Peninsula, and formed a part of the reserve troops, commanded by Major General G. W. Smith, which brought up the rear in the famous retreat from Yorktown. The regiment commanded by Colonel E. L. Thomas, was first engaged in action at Seven Pines, on the 30th May, 1862, being a portion of the force which attacked the right of the enemy, and retired at the termination of the engagement with a loss of twenty-three killed and fifty wounded. Among the number of the slain we had to mourn our gallant Lieutenant Colonel G. A. Bull. At Mechanicsville the Thirty-fifth formed a part of Brigadier General Anderson's force, and commanded by Colonel Thomas accompanied that brigade in its charge on the enemy's position near Mechanicsville, on the 26th of June, 1862, maintaining the unequal conflict until night, and sustaining a loss of eighteen killed and sixty-one wounded. In the list of killed was the Adjutant, J. H. Ware, and among the wounded were Colonel Thomas, and Captain L. P. Thomas, the Regimental Quartermaster. In the other engagements around Richmond, it accompanied A. P. Hill's light Division and performed the part required of it with honor to itself, being commanded by Captain Groves, of Company I. The casualties in these successive actions amounted to three killed and thirteen wounded. In the latter part of July the Light Division was transferred to Jackson's command, and as the engagement of Cedar Run, fought August 9th, 1862, was the next of that noble chieftains victories, this regiment commanded by Major Holt, was there, being on the extreme right of the line. This was the first field fight in which the Thirty-fifth Georgia had been engaged, and nobly did it perform its duty, assisting to repel every attempt of the enemy to turn our right flank. This signal victory elated the spirits of the men beyond measure. The casualties of the regiment in this engagement amounted to nine killed and seventeen wounded.

In Jackson's famous campaign, succeeding this battle, Thomas' Brigade participated and the Thirty-fifth accompanied the brigade in its march to Manassas, witnessed the destruction of the trains captured there by General Stuart, marched to Centreville, retraced its steps to Manassas, and was there formed in line of battle, supporting General Ewell's Division in the action of Thursday, August 31st, 1862. On the 29th it occupied a position on the railroad and sustained the assault of the enemy in front, until late in the evening when the enemy broke through a gap in the line, thereby flanking and forcing the brigade back a short distance. The greater portion of the regiment soon rallied, and accompanied Pender in his splendid charge on that day. On the ensuing day the regiment was again on the line of battle, and advanced with it on the enemy driving them from the field. The loss sustained in these three days engagements amounted to eighteen killed and fifty-five wounded.

At Ox Hill one man was wounded during that engagement, although the regiment was not actively engaged yet exposed to a severe fire. Likewise at Harper's Ferry the loss was slight, being four wounded while it supported Pender, and entered the town with his brigade immediately on its surrender. Here the regiment remained three days to prevent incursions of the enemy, and guarding the vast quantity of military stores captured there, until they were removed; hence it did not recross into Maryland again, but was at Shepherdstown covering the crossing of our army at that place, and lost in the engagement at that point nine wounded. The Thirty-fifth assisted to tear up the Baltimore and Ohio railroad, near Harper's Ferry in October, 1862, and picketed at Summit Point and Snicker's Gap, thence marching to Fredericksburg and bearing a very prominent part in that disastrous repulse of the enemy on the 13th of December, losing fourteen killed and forty-one wounded. In all these engagements from Richmond to Maryland, and back to the Rappahannock, the Thirty-fifth commanded by Major Holt, excepting on the 30th of March, by Captain Groves, performed its duty faithfully, and assisted to give Thomas' Brigade the enviable reputation it acquired in that campaign.

Various changes had been made during the campaign among the officers by promotions, deaths and resignations. Colonel Thomas had fought his way up to the position of Brigadier General. Major Holt was now Colonel, Captain McCulloh of Company K, Lieutenant Colonel, and Captain Groves, Company I, Major. The regiment spent its second winter in Virginia very pleasantly, near Guinea's Station. Picket duty was light and the men were accustomed to camp life, while high hopes of going home on a visit were indulged in, and by many happily realized.

With the disappearance of winter came the disappearance of winter quarters. Hooker crossed the Rappahannock and commenced fortifying within twelve miles of the centre of the Army of Northern Virginia. Such audacity must needs be punished, which resulted in the battle of Chancellorsville, May 3d, 1863, in which action the Thirty-fifth commanded by Captain Duke, Company A, was engaged, charging the enemy from their position, driving them over a mile, taking their breastworks, and capturing many prisoners, with a loss of eight killed and twenty-seven wounded.

Lieutenant General Jackson's services having been lost to the Confederacy by his untimely death, Major General Hill was promoted, and Major General Pender was assigned to the command of the Light Division, now reduced to four brigades–Archer's and Fields' brigades having been withdrawn from it.

A lull succeeded the storm, but the waves arose again early in June, 1863, at which time Hooker crossed a portion of his command on the east bank of the Rappahannock. Pender's Division took position in line of battle at Hamilton's Crossing, forming the right of the line, remaining here ten days awaiting an attack of the enemy, and then began to march to Pennsylvania. The weather was exceedingly warm, and the three first days march the men suffered severely from heat, many falling down fainting by the road side. After this, however, the men were not marched so far in a day nor in such haste, the beneficial effects of which change was very visible in the Thirty-fifth thereafter. Marching and camping were the business of nearly every day, until the vicinity of Gettysburg was reached. On the morning of the 1st of July, 1863, the Thirty-fifth was detached to guard a wagon train. It was known a battle was imminent, and it was presumed that this regiment would take no part in it; but after an hour's stay with the wagons an order was received to join the brigade, which we proceeded to do, running for nearly three miles and getting into position, as the batteries of the enemy opened on that part of the lines. Placed as was the brigade, between the corps' of Ewell and Hill to hold the centre and prevent the former from being outflanked on the right, and the latter on the left, and supporting a heavy battery the regiment had nothing to do save dodging shells and witnessing the first day's engagement.

On the second day the regiment, with the exception of three companies, were deployed as skirmishers, and from the losses sustained showed that the skirmish fight in front of Pender's Division was the most fierce on record. Charge after charge was made, and in one assault the skirmishers advanced within a short distance of the enemy's batteries. The night of the 2d of July, Thomas' Brigade took a position in a hollow between the opposing lines, and on the next morning the greater part of the regiment was again deployed, keeping up a line equal in length to the front of two brigades, and continuing the action. When the grand charge was made some brigade in its advance passed near Thomas' Brigade and seemed disposed to stop;

but that it might have no excuse for halting, General Thomas ordered his brigade forward. The Thirty-fifth being near him heard the command and led by Lieutenant Colonel McCulloh, participated in that ever memorable charge of Picket and Heth. Night closed the scene, and on the 5th of July the regiment bade farewell to Pennsylvania, and fell back to Hagerstown and there remained in line of battle several days, finally crossing the Potomac with the army into Virginia. The casualties in the battle of Gettysburg amounted to nine killed, fifty-three wounded and fifty-seven missing. Total loss one hundred and nineteen.

The regiment accompanied the brigade to Orange Court House. In the advance to Bristol Station it experienced the same treatment as at Gettysburg, respecting guarding wagon trains, and again retired across the Rapidan. When Meade crossed the Potomac and was met at Mine Run, the regiment was there though not actively engaged, often changing positions to meet the attempts of the enemy to turn our right. Only two were wounded here.

Winter quarters had been erected for 1863, and as they were about to be occupied, Averill made a descent upon the Virginia and Tennessee railroad, and the brigade of General Thomas was ordered to the Valley of Virginia to intercept him. During the most severe part of the winter the regiment proceeded to Millboro; but Averill having gone another route and Boyd having ascended the Valley, making a diversion in Averill's favor, we were countermarched to Staunton and commenced the race after Boyd. The regiment left camp near Staunton at three o'clock, A.M., and traveled to Lorey Springs, thirty-seven miles distant, in a continuous march, reaching that place on the evening of the same day, but Boyd was too quick for Early.

The most of the winter was spent in running up and down the Valley and feasting on the fat of the land. A trip across the mountains was made to Moorfield and Petersburg; but the enemy fled, leaving behind him his cattle and many valuable military stores. After the winter was over the regiment enjoyed themselves finely for awhile near Harrisonburg, Virginia, but soon this "foot cavalry" was ordered to rejoin the "parent body," and a five days march found them at Orange Court House, among old and tried friends in Wilcox's Division–Major General Wilcox having succeeded to the command of the Light Division on the demise of General Pender.

The only changes that occurred among the commissioned officers during this winter, were the promotions of Captain Williams to Major. Captain Steed to the command of Company C, Captain Mitchell to Company D, and Captain Roberts to Company H.

On the 4th of May, 1864, General U. S. Grant, then commanding the Federal forces, commenced crossing the disputed line, and was promptly met by the Army of Northern Virginia in the Wilderness. There on the plank road where Grant had massed his troops on the 5th of May, Heth and Wilcox sustained the furious assault of the enemy, maintaining their position under the heaviest fire of musketry ever witnessed on this continent. When night closed the fight against such overwhelming odds, our line was necessarily slightly disarranged, and Longstreet being expected to relieve the line before the break of day, only the customary vigilance was used during the night. Fatal neglect! When morning dawned, Thomas' noble and as yet invincible brigade was almost totally enveloped in the dense masses of the enemy, who in numbers comparing to ours twenty to one, were threatening our front, flank and rear. For awhile we stood unshaken, but while attempting to execute under a fearfully galling fire, the manoeuvre of "into line faced to the rear," the regiment fell back to its supports in confusion, and were not rallied until supports were brought up. The losses of the regiment in the two days engagements amounted to four killed, twenty-two wounded and twenty-three missing.

Again at Spottsylvania on the 12th of May, the regiment participated in retaking the works lost by Johnson's Division, supporting Gordon's Brigade in its charge across the breastworks, and losing ten killed, thirty-seven wounded and fifteen missing. Major Williams was here mortally wounded, and died on the 18th of May.

At Jericho Ford, having been sent in to gobble up a handful of cavalry, it found itself, after advancing one-fourth of a mile, fronting Warren's entire corps of Yankees, whose rear was protected by twenty or thirty pieces of artillery, on the heights across the river, and which vomited innumerable shell and canister among the devoted band of Southerners there present. The division being unable to capture the entire corps, withdrew after night, with a loss to the Thirty-fifth Georgia of ten killed, twenty-eight wounded and twenty-one missing.

At Hames' Shop, June 14th, some more cavalry were to be driven back, which was successfully done after a severe skirmish fight, in which the Thirty-fifth lost two killed and six wounded.

Grant having crossed the James, the regiment, after a severe march reached Petersburg and took position on the Weldon railroad.

A reconnoisance in force was made on the 21st of June in front of our position, which succeeded in driving the enemy to his breastworks, and on the succeeding day Thomas' Brigade aided, by a detour to the rear of the enemy, in withdrawing him from his position, and afterwards supported the attacking column, on the enemy's flank, by which position his guns and many of his men were captured. The loss in the Thirty-fifth was three wounded and three missing.

On the line of battle, commanded by Lieutenant Colonel McCulloh, the regiment still remains fronting the foes of our country with undiminished ardor, undimmed patriotism, and unabated zeal, ever ready to spring to arms and strike another and another blow for the inalienable right of self government. We are quietly reposing in our comfortless quarters, but whoever ventures to disturb our repose will bitterly repent it, for not lethargic sleep is upon us, and we are ready, willing and anxious to again try the issue by the strength of arms, and thus end the strife.

The losses of the regiment will be found at the head of this chapter, but if to that list were added those who are disabled by wounds, but not discharged, and the number now missing, the total loss would approximate two-thirds of all who have ever belonged to it.

So closes the drama of the actions of the Thirty-fifth Georgia regiment, and here let the curtain fall until a new scene shall be presented, in which the few of this regiment now fit for duty will be prominent actors, and we doubt not that each member will perform his part as faithfully as in the past, so that the regimental pride shall not be lowered, or that the laurels it has gained upon seventeen gory fields be removed from its banners. The narrow limits allowed prevent a notice of all the promotions among the officers, and the changes wrought by death and wounds, nor has it been possible to note the many instances of gallantry discharged by different members of this command. While they are unwritten they are not unknown, and it is confidently hoped that a record of their achievements will be published, so that posterity yet unborn shall delight to dwell upon the deeds of valor and heroism performed by those who sacrificed for home all its endearments, and for freedom that which man may take but cannot give.

GEORGIA VOLUNTEERS

STATISTICAL RECORD.

STRENGTH OF REGIMENT.

Number of men originally enlisted, ...	769
" " recruits, ...	328
Total strength, ...	1097

LOSSES BY DEATH.

Killed in action, ...	138
Died of disease, ...	212
Total of deaths, ...	350

LOSSES OTHERWISE THAN BY DEATH.

Discharged, ...	178
Wounded, ...	436
Total of all losses, ...	954

The Fourteenth Georgia Regiment was organized in the city of Atlanta, Georgia, on the 17th of July, 1861, to serve three years or during the war; and was composed of the following companies:

Company A, from Monroe County, Captain John H. Etheridge.
Company B, from Wilkinson County, Captain Robert W. Folsom.
Company C, from Jasper County, Captain C. W. Jordon.
Company D, from Cherokee County, Captain James M. Fielder.
Company E, from Forsyth County, Captain R. P. Lester.
Company F, from Johnson County, Captain R. P. Harmon.
Company G, from Worth County, Captain William A. Harris.
Company H, from Lawrens County, Captain J. S. Ramsey.
Company I, from Butler County, Captain Felix Price.
Company K, from Bartow County, Captain Thomas S. Jones.

A. V. Brumby, of Marietta, was elected Colonel; Captain J. S. Ramsey was elected Lieutenant Colonel; Captain Felix Price was elected Major; and Lieutenant A. D. Hammond, Company A, was appointed Adjutant; Dr. Young was appointed Surgeon; W. J. Williford, Quartermaster; and Henry C. Kellogg, Commissary. Lieutenant T. M. Yopp was elected Captain to fill the vacancy left by promotion of Captain Ramsey. Lieutenant Rufus W. McMichael was elected Captain to fill the vacancy left by promotion of Captain Price.

On the 18th and 19th of July the regiment left Atlanta, and went by way of Knoxville, Tennessee, to Lynchburg, Virginia, where it remained about ten days, and was then ordered to Staunton. From Staunton we marched by way of Monterey to Huntersville, in Pocahontas County, remained there about three weeks and moved to Marlin Bottom, on the Green Brier river. Remaining but a few days at the latter place we again moved, going to Edray, a short distance beyond, and from that place to Tygarts Valley, on the head waters of the Elk river. Shortly after reaching this place the enemy, under General Rosecrans, moved down on the Gauly river, and General Lee withdrew his forces, the Fourteenth Georgia falling back with the army to Green Brier river.

General Loring in command of the greater portion of the army, went down on the Gauly river, and the remainder left at Marlin's Bottom were under the command of General Donaldson, of Tennessee–an officer long to be remembered for his kindness and courtesy. This was our first campaign remarkable in the history of the regiment for the sickness and sufferings we endured. We were *raw men*, ignorant of camp life, unused to exposures of wet and cold, and the fatigues of marching. We were encumbered with many things useless to the old soldier, and destitute of others since learned to be indispensable. We had to undergo the sickness always incident to camp life, and the season was an unusually wet one. Measels and mumps broke out and quickly spread through every company. While laboring under these diseases many took cold, and added to this, fever of a most malignant form made its appearance to an alarming extent. The medical department was unorganized, the supply of medicine wholly inadequate, and the accommodations for the sick of the very poorest kind. The consequence was disease and death were spread out on every hand. We left Lynchburg in the latter part of July, seven hundred and seventy strong, and of this number but one hundred and twenty reported for duty. Among the officers who died, were Dr. Young and Lieutenants Birge, Hunt and Weeks.

During this campaign Lieutenant Colonel Ramsey resigned, and Captain Folsom was elected to fill the vacancy. Lieutenant C. C. Kelly was elected Captain; Second Lieutenant W. J. Solomon was elected First, and John McArthur, Brevet Second Lieutenant; First Lieutenant Haupt resigned and Lieutenant Mays elected to fill his place, and Jeff Hogan elected Brevet Second Lieutenant; Lieutenant Ward resigned and J. O. Lane filled the vacancy. The death of Lieutenant Hunt leaving a vacancy, it was filled by Lieutenant McConnel, and Lieutenant Abbott and W. D. Putnam promoted, Lieutenant Seal resigned and W. H. Paxton was elected Brevet Second Lieutenant. Lieutenant Kent resigned and J. W. Crawford filled his place by election. Lieutenant Geddeon resigned and Lieutenant Weeks died, their places were filled by the election of Terrell T. Monger and John R. Bozeman. Lieutenants Rowe, Hall and Duffy resigned and P. W. Douglas, D. W. Patterson and John F. Davis were elected. Captain Jones and Lieutenant Fields resigned, and Lieutenant Birge died, Lieutenant Goldsmith was elected Captain and R. A. Holt, James Jackson, and T. C. Moore were elected Second Lieutenants. Thus in the course of three months, there were *four deaths and ten resignations* among the commissioned officers of the regiment. The proportion of deaths and discharges among the enlisted men were equally as great.

In the latter part of October the regiment marched to Millboro, on the Virginia Central railroad, and from there proceeded to Manassas Junction, where it joined the Army of Northern Virginia, under General Joseph E. Johnston. We went into camp on the railroad just below the depot, and were employed on guard and fatigue duty until about Christmas, when we were ordered to Davis' Ford on the Ocoquan, where we again went into camp. While at Manassas Colonel Brumby resigned his commission and Major Price was elected to fill the vacancy, Lieutenant Colonel Folsom refusing to become a candidate.

Captain Jordan resigned and Lieutenant L. A. Lane was elected Captain, and W. J. Preston, First Lieutenant Acting Adjutant; Lieutenant Hammock resigned and James Jordan was elected Brevet Second Lieutenant of Company A; Lieutenant Chappell resigned and I. C. Perry was elected. Captain Williford resigned and E. A. Heggie was appointed quartermaster. Captain Kelloggg resigned and Captain R. P. Harman was detailed in his place. A. Taliferro was appointed Adjutant.

While at Davis' Ford the regiment was engaged in building forts and digging rifle pits. We were here placed in General Wade Hampton's Brigade, Whiting's Division. At this place Captain Harris was elected Major, to fill the vacancy occasioned by the election of Major Price to the Colonelcy. Lieutenant Monger became Captain, and Robert F. Shine was elected First Lieutenant; R. N. Ryle was elected Second Lieutenant to fill the vacancy left by Lieutenant Linge, who had resigned. Captain Harman was relieved from duty as Commissary and Lieutenant Moore was detailed for that duty. During the whole of this winter the regiment lived in tents. On the 7th of March, 1863, we broke up camp, and with the remainder of the division marched to Fredericksburg, where we remained enjoying the hospitalities of that ancient and once famous town (now dispoiled of its wealth and beauty by the hand of a cruel enemy,) until the 8th of April, when we took up the line of march for Yorktown. We left Yorktown on the 5th of May, and marched to the vicinity of Richmond. Our first battle was that of Seven Pines. Unfortunately the regiment was put into action late in the evening, just before the close of that hard fought battle. The position attacked by us was an extremely strong one, and the disparity in numbers was greatly in favor of the enemy, much greater no doubt than was supposed by the commanding Generals; but our Brigade (Hampton's) composed of the Fourteenth and Nineteenth Georgia, the Sixteenth North Carolina, and Hampton's Infantry Battalion, was ordered into action upon this strongly fortified line. The first and only order given after the formation of our line of battle was to charge, and the movement was executed in fine style, until we advanced into the woods filled with a dense undergrowth. Here the line became broken, but continued to advance until within less than fifty paces of the enemy's line, and immediately in front of one of his strongest batteries. At this moment the batteries of the enemy belched forth their thunders, showering a perfect hail storm of canister and grape into our lines, while a withering fire of musketry was poured upon us. An order to lie down was given, and it was then discovered that we were being flanked. Having no supports, or they not bring up, the result was that the whole brigade retreated in disorder. It was rallied and again and again led to the assault with other troops, but the numbers and position of the enemy were too strong for us, and although the fighting continued until after dark, we failed to force the enemy from the field. It was on this part of the battle ground and during these operations that General Joseph E. Johnston received his wound. Here the regiment lost Captain John H. Etheridge. Before the war Captain Etheridge was a practicing physician in Monroe County. He was a man of fine personal appearance, engaging manners, and of high standing socially and professionally. As an officer he was kind, conscientious and efficient. His company were greatly attached to him, and his death was universally regretted in the regiment. Lieutenant Shine was also killed. He was an amiable young man and much beloved by his company. The regiment lost in all ten killed and twenty-eight wounded.

Shortly after the battle of Seven Pines, the regiment was placed in a brigade commanded by the gallant General Archer, but before the battle of Mechanicsville was fought, a Georgia Brigade composed of the Fourteenth, Thirty-fifth, Forty-fifth and Forty-ninth Georgia Regiments was formed, and General Joseph R. Anderson, of Richmond, placed in command of it. The organization of this brigade has remained unchanged to the present time. It was then attached to General A. P. Hill's Light Division, which has subsequently earned a fame which will live through all time. The regiment participated in all the "battles around Richmond," beginning at Mechanicsville, and ending at Malvern Hill. It is needless to say that it acquitted itself with honor, never faltering in the hottest of the many charges made upon the strong works of McClellan. During these engagements Lieutenant James Jordan was wounded and afterwards died in Richmond, Lieutenant J. W. Mays was made Captain; Lieutenants Hogan and Merrit were promoted, and Hiram Perdue was made Lieutenant. The loss of the regiment in these battles was twenty-four killed and sixty wounded.

The regiment had scarcely rested from its severe duties in front of Richmond, when it was again put in motion and sent to Gordonsville where it joined the forces of the lamented Stonewall, under whom it marched and fought up to the time of his untimely death.

The next battle of the regiment was Cedar Run, in which Lieutenant Colonel Robert W. Folsom, greatly distinguished himself. At that time his health was extremely feeble. The day was an unusually hot one, and the march had been long and fatiguing. While the regiment were charging the enemy and supporting a brigade in its front, that brigade suddenly gave way, and retreated in great confusion through the lines of the Fourteenth. The regiment wavered and in a moment would have been in headlong route; but at the critical moment, when nothing apparently could retrieve the threatened disaster, Lieutenant Colonel Folsom sprang forward and seizing the battle-grimed colors of the Fourteenth, rushed forward and in a voice whose intonations rang far over the plain, called upon the Fourteenth, "for the sake of old Georgia to stand!" The panic ceased, and calling upon his gallant boys to "follow their Colonel," he pressed forward, but had not proceeded far when exhausted nature gave way and he fell prostrate overcome by the heat and feebleness. Raising himself, and supported on either side by brave and devoted comrades, he again advanced fully thirty paces in front of his regiment. His men seeing his courage and determination, caught the inspiration of his spirit and rushed to his side. The charge was continued, the enemy fled, and victory perched upon the banner so nobly, gallantly and heroically borne.

During this engagement the Fourteenth charged and utterly routed three times their numbers, and received and repulsed a desperate charge of the enemy's cavalry; and were said by General Hill, to have killed and wounded as many of the enemy as their own strength amounted to, and yet, through the protection of an Allwise Providence, their loss was but one killed and nine wounded.

After the battle of Cedar Run, we marched back to the neighborhood of Orange Court House, where General Jackson rested his corps until the main army under General Lee came up from Richmond. We then marched through Culpepper county to Jeffersonton. Here the corps of General Jackson left the main army and commenced that brilliant flank movement on the enemy, then occupying a line along the north side of the Rappahannock. Bearing to the left, passing through the villages of Orleans and Salem, by a rapid march General Jackson reached Manassas Junction and Bristol Station, before the enemy were aware that he had left the banks of the Rappahannock. Stonewall was then directly in their rear and on their line of communication, with Alexandria their base of supplies.

At no period in the history of the war, has the indomitable spirit and cheerfulness of the soldiers of the army of Northern

Virginia, under trying circumstances, been more forcibly illustrated than on the march to Bristol Station. The rations consisted of flour and fresh beef alone. These were generally issued late at night, when the troops were weary, foot sore and sleepy. They were to be cooked, divided, and in the haversacks before day, and by light the line of march was generally resumed. In consequence the rations were not more than half cooked and greatly wasted. Being scanty at best, it is easy to imagine that the men suffered from hunger. The marches were hard and continued until late at night; many of the men were barefoot, and all were dirty and ragged; yet they maintained their cheerfulness, and in the still hours of the night, the solitude of the fields and forests were awakened by the sounds of songs and merry laughter as the troops marched on, following their great leader.

At Manassas an immense quantity of stores, consisting in great part of commissary supplies were captured. As it was thought best to destroy all the men could not carry with them, they were allowed to help themselves. Every man in the regiment filled his haversack with pickled beef, bacon or pork, sugar and coffee, and took whatever else pleased him. This was to the worn out, half-starved men, a real God-send–every man felt that he carried a feast. When all was helped, what remained, to the value of millions, was burnt.

Early next morning we marched to Centerville, and from thence to the field of the *second battle of Manassas*. This certainly was one of the hardest fought battles, and most glorious victories to the Confederate arms, which had then occurred. The Fourteenth did its full and honorable part in this severe and bloody battle. The ground in front of its position was literally strewn with the blue coats; and it was here called upon to mourn the death of some of its bravest members. Captain Rufus W. McMichael here lost his life. He fell in the thickest of the fight, nobly performing his part in the securing of his country's liberty. He was just entering upon a life, to him, full of bright prospects and radient with buoyant hopes; but fate decreed that he should yield up all, and he offered his all–his arms were forced, in grief, to leave him behind. The loss of the regiment in this engagement was eight killed and thirty-one wounded.

The next engagement in which the Fourteenth was engaged, was that of Ox Hill or Chantilly, from which it marched by way of Leesburg into Maryland. After crossing the Potomac the first meal eaten by this regiment consisted of green corn, roasted. This was issued as the only ration that could be furnished. The next day we marched to Monocacy bridge, near Frederick City, Maryland. We marched from here (in a few days after our arrival,) by way of Middletown and Boonsboro, to Williamsport, crossed the Potomac and proceeded to Martinsburg, where we captured a quantity of military supplies, and from thence marched to Harper's Ferry. We here captured nearly thirteen thousand prisoners and an immense quantity of supplies. Here again we were feasted at the expense of "Abe's best government," &c. The brigade was posted at this place as a guard, while the battle of Sharpsburg was being fought. Shortly afterwards we were engaged at Shepherdstown, and afterwards went into camp near Bunker Hill, where it remained several months.

While at Bunker Hill Lieutenant Colonel Folsom was promoted to Colonel–Colonel Price having resigned. It is due to the memory of Colonel Folsom to state, that he commanded the regiment in the battle of Cedar Run and in all subsequent engagements. Capt. Fielder was promoted Major, to fill the vacancy occasioned by the resignation of Major Harris, on account of a wound. Lieutenant McConnel was promoted Captain; Lieutenants Abbot and Putnam, and James L. Hull were promoted; Robert H. Fulton was promoted First Lieutenant, and Jas. H. Ford to Second, to fill the vacancies of Lieutenant Shine killed and Bostick died. Lieutenant Moore was commissioned A. C. S. In the latter part of November the army marched to Fredericksburg, where the enemy were concentrating a large army.

On the 13th of December the battle of Fredericksburg was fought, in which the Fourteenth under its gallant commander took a nobly conspicuous part. Unprotected by breastworks, it repulsed three heavy lines of battle. The loss of the regiment in the battle was severe, being twenty-four killed and eighty-eight wounded. Among the former was Lieutenant Washington J. Solomon, a gallant and amiable young officer, whose loss was deeply deplored; also Lieutenant Putnam, a noble, chivalric officer. The regiment shortly after this battle, went into winter quarters at Camp Gregg, about ten miles below Fredericksburg. While in winter quarters Major Fielder was promoted to Lieutenant Colonel, and Captain Lester was promoted to Major.[*] During the preceding campaign Lieutenant Hogan lost an eye and resigned, and Lieutenant Johnson died.

In May, 1863, the battle of Chancellorsville was fought, from which the regiment had to mourn the loss of Lieutenant Colonel

---

[*] Owing to want of space I am compelled to expunge the list of promotions which has been forwarded to me.

Fielder, Captains Mounger and Harmon, and Lieutenant H. A. Solomon.

Lieutenant Colonel Fielder, though over the military age, entered the service at the beginning of the war, impelled by his love of country and zeal for the cause of liberty. He possessed, in a remarkable degree, the confidence, love and esteem of the regiment–fortitude, devotion and constancy, characterized his military life. A kinder, more benevolent heart never beat. All his purposes were high, honorable and christianlike. His friendship was true, disinterested and constant. As a citizen at home, he stood deservedly high. He met his fate as becomes a soldier and a christian, with fortitude and a well grounded faith in the merits and mercy of his Redeemer. Long, long will the surviving members of the Fourteenth cherish in love the memory of his name.

Captain Mounger was a physician when the war began, and entered the service as a private in the Fourth Georgia Regiment, and was afterwards elected to a position in the Fourteenth. He was a general favorite in the regiment, and his company was devotedly attached to him. He was of a sanguine temperament, polite in his deportment, generous and social, being at all times a favorite with any with whom he had dealings. His sensibilities were of the highest and most delicate order. As an officer he was prompt and exact, but kind and just to those under his command. In action his bravery was of that cool, lofty, determined, and vigorous order, which inspires the beholder with admiration and enthusiasm. He died as he had lived, universally beloved by officers and men. A little mound upon the battle field of Chancellorsville is all that marks his resting place, but his comrades will ever cherish his memory.

Lieutenant Henry A. Solomon entered the service in the First Georgia Regiment. He afterwards served in the army of the west, and upon the death of his gallant, noble hearted brother, (Lieutenant W. J. Solomon,) who fell at the battle of Fredericksburg, he was elected to fill the vacancy. He was brave to rashness, generous to a fault, kind and sympathising as a friend. His brother was possessed of all his good qualities, but his courage was of that stubborn, unyielding nature which could with stand defeat, without the depression usually consequent upon disaster.

As an example of the fortitude of Captain Mounger and Lieutenant H. A. Solomon, it is said, that they walked in company with each other for three miles after receiving their mortal wounds. The former shot through and through the bowels; the latter shot clear through the body–the ball perforating in its passage, both lungs and liver.

The regiment accompanied the army into Pennsylvania, and was engaged in the battle of Gettysburg; sustaining in that terrific engagement, a loss of eleven (11) killed and thirty-three (33) wounded. Subsequently, we fell back with the army to the neighborhood of Bunker Hill, and from thence to Orange Court House, where it arrived about the first of August. Major Lester was here promoted to Lieutenant Colonel; Captain Goldsmith to Major, and Lieutenant Holt to Captain of Company K. Lieutenant Jackson having previously resigned, G. W. Chapman was elected in his place.

In the month of October the regiment marched with its division to Bristol Station, and was at Mine Run, but was not engaged. After this we went into winter quarters near Orange Court House.

On the 15th of December, shortly after having completed their winter cabins, the regiment was ordered to Staunton, and was placed under the command of General Early, commanding in the Valley. The remainder of the winter of 1863 and 1864, was spent in marching and countermarching up and down the Valley, as far as New Town and to Petersburg, in Hardy county. The season was intensely cold, and the command being destitute of tents, were compelled to bivouac in the open air, frequently on snow and ice. Under every hardship the men maintained their usual cheerfulness. In February, 1864, we rejoined the main army at Orange Court House, where we remained until the spring campaign opened.

On the 5th of May the Fourteenth with other portions of the army, became engaged with the enemy in the battle of the Wilderness. When the fight ceased at night the line of battle occupied by the Fourteenth was very irregular, and during the night the enemy taking advantage of this irregularity, so disposed their lines as to be able next morning to attack our position in front, flank and rear. Colonel Folsom perceived the danger of his position, and the utter impossibility of holding the line. He did all in his power to have the line corrected, but it was not done. During the whole night the officers and men of the Fourteenth felt that they were doomed to a useless and terrible danger, and that the morrow's sun would shine upon the lifeless bodies of many of their number. Early the next morning the shock fell with terrible force upon the Fourteenth, but it maintained its position, fighting with the resolution of despair the formidable host which had nearly surrounded it; but slowly the overpowering forces of the enemy moved around, until we were almost within their clutches, when the order to fall back was given, and Colonel Folsom attempted to carry out his regiment in order. Before he could accomplish this attempt a ball struck him, and passing through the upper part of his stomach inflicted a mortal wound. He was taken to the field hospital, where, after suffering for thirty-two hours his noble heart ceased to beat, and his spirit winged its flight to Heaven.

No officer of equal rank in the army of Northern Virginia, enjoyed a more enviable reputation and position, than did Colonel Robert W. Folsom at his death. None had better deserved that reputation and position than he. To bravery of the most daring kind, he united the calmest, most imperturbable coolness, and the most circumspect caution. His judgment was solid, and always matured from a careful review of all the surrounding circumstances; and he possessed the energy and steadfastness of character to follow the dictates of that judgment. He was eminently qualified to govern men; commanding their respect, and binding them to him at the same time with the chords of affection. As a disciplinarian he was rigid, but scrupulously just. In his intercourse with both officers and men he was courteous and kind. His attention to the business of the regiment was unremitting and energetic. His administrative abilities were of the highest order. As a messmate he was social, agreeable, liberal and instructive. He loved and venerated truth, justice and sincerity. He never exercised a petty tyranny, or assumed a false dignity on account of position and power, instances of which are so common and so disgusting in the army. So widespread was his reputation, that General Lee has highly complimented him in an order written with his own hand and signed by himself, and now in possession of the Colonel's family.

In the fall of 1863, a Military Lodge of Free and Accepted Masons was established in this brigade, of which Colonel Folsom was the Worshipful Master. He retained this place, discharging its duties up to the time of his death. He was a bright and zealous Mason, exemplifying the great moral teachings of the order in his daily walk and in his death it may be truly said, the fraternity lost "a true and worthy brother." As a professor of religion he was devoted, sincere and consistent, and in the latter part of his life was particularly zealous. His religion was not of the sombre puritanical caste, but bright, cheerful and hopeful. At the time of his death he was in the very prime and vigor of manhood, being but twenty-eight years of age. His last hours were characterized by the most perfect submission to the will of God, and the most confiding faith in his acceptance with his Heavenly Father. There did not seem to be a cloud to obstruct his vision; but with songs of praise and rejoicing, the young and promising hero entered the dark valley and shadow of death with the rod and staff of his Redeemer to comfort and support him.

The regiment has participated in the battles around Spottsylvania Court House, also at Jericho Ford, and in several engagements, and has lost severely. Among the killed are Captains S. B. David and R. A. Holt, and Lieutenants Patterson and Chapman.

Lieutenant Colonel Lester has been promoted to Colonel; Major Goldsmith to Lieutenant Colonel, and Captain C. C. Kelly to Major; Lieutenant Ryles to Captain, also Lieutenants Rogers and Eaves; Lieutenants McAfee and Goldsmith promoted. Captain Clegg retired on account of disability and Lieutenant Ilicks promoted to Captain; Lieutenants McVay and Lumley promoted. Captain Smith was retired, and Lieutenant Perry promoted to Captain; D. H. McLendon to First Lieutenant, and J. W. Jones to Brevet Second Lieutenant. Adjutant Taliaferro was retired, and Captain T. C. Moore, formerly Assistant Commissary of Subsistence of the regiment was appointed Adjutant.

Among the heroes of this gallant regiment I present the name of J. Rufus Kelly, of Company B, from Wilkinson county. During the engagement at Jericho Ford, one of the regiments of this brigade suddenly giving way, caused such confusion in the Fourteenth that it was ordered back, when young Kelly, but eighteen years of age, seeing them falling back in disorder, and thinking it was panic, suddenly rushed forward about thirty yards in front of the regiment, his rifle in his left hand, his hat swinging over his head in the right, he called upon the regiment to stand; but they heeded him not, and proudly refusing to follow the regiment, he joined another brigade as a volunteer and went into the fight, but had hardly become engaged when he received a wound in his leg which necessitated immediate amputation. He little knew that at the distance of scarce a mile, the body of his Colonel (Folsom) was being borne to a southern grave; that Colonel, who, at Cedar Run, had set him an example which at Jericho Ford he had so nobly followed.

Henry and Solomon Goodman, two young German brothers of Company B, deserve a special notice; not only for bravery and coolness when in action, but for their loyalty to their adopted country, under circumstances which would try the loyalty of almost any one who have not that devoted love of country which only birth can give. The families of these youths have cruelly deserted them and gone North, carrying with them all the property left in their keeping by these boys, and left them to their fate. Their coolness and courage is proverbial in the Fourteenth Georgia; and although no particular act of courage can be specified, still it is a pleasure to honor and praise where honor and praise are due.

GEORGIA VOLUNTEERS

(SAVANNAH VOLUNTEER GUARDS)

———

STATISTICAL REPORT.

Number of men originally enlisted, ...	279
Number of volunteer recruits, (no conscripts), ...	177
Total strength, ...	456

LOSSES.

Number of men killed in action, ...	8
Number of men died of disease, ...	20
Total deaths, ...	28
Number of men discharged, ...	60
Number of men deserted, ...	23
Number of men transferred, ...	48
Total loss, ...	159
Number of men wounded in action, ...	8

The Eighteenth Battalion of Georgia Volunteers is a volunteer corps of the city of Savannah, and was organized in the year 1862, and was known as the Savannah Volunteer Guards.

When it was deemed advisable by the governor of Georgia to take possession of Fort Pulaski, the Guards, then a single company, was a part of the force designated for that purpose. They were commanded by Captain John Screven. The detachment consisted besides this company, of the Oglethorpe Light Infantry, Captain F. S. Bartow, and the Chatham Artillery, Captain J. S. Claghorn. All these companies then belonged to the First Volunteer Regiment, commanded by Colonel A. R. Lawton, who was in command of the expedition.

Fort Pulaski continued to be garrisoned by the volunteer troops of Savannah until it was turned over to the Confederate government,–the different companies alternating, two or three at a time, in performing that duty. During this interval the Guards organized a second company. For a long time even before a spark of war appeared, the accession to their ranks had been so numerous, that it became evident that it would be necessary to expand their organization. On their second tour of duty at the Fort, they went with two companies so large that they alone were considered sufficient for its garrison.

When it appeared that war was inevitable, and the government began to erect fortifications upon the coast, the volunteer troops of Savannah were called upon to enter the service of the Confederacy for short periods of time. The guards were enlisted June 1st, 1861, for two months,–Company A, Captain John Screven; Company B, Captain A. C. Davenport. The battalion, under command of Captain Screven, was ordered on duty at Thunderbolt battery, about five miles from Savannah, where it remained during the whole period of its enlistment.

The two companies were again mustered into service for six months from September 1st, 1861, and ordered to duty at Fort Screven on Green Island, near the mouth of the Great Ogechee. This was a heavy battery of ten guns, including some of the greatest calibre then known in the service. Here both officers and men acquired a considerable degree of skill as artillerists, which influenced in a very great degree the character of their subsequent service. At this place the companies numbered over one hundred men each; Company A was commanded by Lieutenant Basinger, Company B, by Lieutenant Stiles. Captain Screven commanded the whole. Long before the expiration of this period of enlistment, it has become evident that the Confederacy had embarked in a war, of which the termination could not be foreseen. Both officers and men, therefore, determined to enlist at once for the war, whatever might be its duration; and they did so on March 1st, 1862.

Up to this time the two companies had continued to belong to the First Volunteer Regiment of Georgia* above referred to; but it was generally desired in the command that it should constitute an independent organization. The number of men disposed to enlist for the war at this time, was not sufficient for more than three companies; but the consent of the Confederate authorities to receive these as a battalion had been obtained, and there seemed no reason to doubt that they would increase in size, so as to permit the organization of other companies from time to time; therefore the Guards took their place in the line of the Confederate army, as a battalion commanded by Major John Screven.

The officers of Company A were Captain W. S. Basinger, First Lieutenant T. F. Screven, Second Lieutenants W. H. King and F. Tupper.

The officers of Company B were Captain George W. Stiles, First Lieutenant E. Padelford, Jr., Second Lieutenants E. A. Castelaw and George D. Smith.

The officers of Company C were Captain G. C. Rice, First Lieutenant G. M. Turner, Second Lieutenants J. R. Dillon and E. Blois.

It would be unjust not to state that the rank and file were largely recruited from several of the counties on the Savannah and Albany, and Atlantic and Gulf railroads, which furnished some of the very best soldiers in the battalion. The battalion did not at this time receive its number, but continued to be known for several months by its original name. It was not until December, 1862, that it was officially styled the Eighteenth Georgia Battalion.

The battalion, having been allowed a respite of thirty days, reassembled under orders on the 1st of April, 1862, for its final entrance upon service. Its first post was at Fort Boggs, which guards the left flank of the defences of Savannah. The armament of this place consisted of two mortars, ten heavy guns and six field pieces. The battalion remained at this point until July, 1863, that is, its duty was at that point; but so insalubrious was climate and air during the greater part of the summer, at this locality, that it was necessary to remove the troops, sometimes to the city itself, and once to the Isle of Hope, about ten miles from the city. The summer of 1862, the greater part of which was spent at Fort Boggs, reduced the command

---

* This regiment was formed before the war, and composed entirely of volunteer companies of Savannah. It had no connection whatever with the First Georgia Regiment whose history commences this work.

greatly. As many as one hundred and forty, out of an aggregate of not more than two hundred and fifty present, were borne on the sick report for several days. The well were only nominally so. Exhausted by agues and malarial fevers of every type, they were in constant expectation of the recurrence of disease. It is believed that but one person in the whole command escaped sickness. It was over twelve months before the effects of this summer could be said to have disappeared. At different times Lieutenant Padelford, a most valuable and highly esteemed officer, and a number of the best non-commissioned officers and soldiers fell victims.

May 10th, 1863, the service of Major Screven being required to conduct the Savannah and Albany, and Atlantic and Gulf railroads of which he had been several years president, he resigned his commission, and Captain Basinger succeeded to the command of the battalion. In Company A, Lieutenant Screven became Captain; Second Lieutenant King, First Lieutenant; and Sergeant P. N. Raynal was elected Junior Second Lieutenant. In Company B, by the death of Lieutenant Padelford on June 7th, 1863, Lieutenant Castelaw became First Lieutenant; and some time afterwards Lieutenant W. E. Gue, previously a sergeant of that company, was elected to the junior commission. In June of that year Major Basinger was sent with his own command and Maxwell's Battery of light artillery, to meet an expected descent of the enemy on the coast of Glynn county, Georgia. After the lapse of several weeks, the enemy not appearing, the command was ordered back to Savannah. At this time the battalion was attached to the brigade of General W. B. Taliaferro.

On the 9th of July a detachment of Taliaferro's Brigade, consisting of the Thirty-second Georgia Regiment, Colonel Harrison; four companies of the First Volunteer Regiment of Georgia, Colonel Olmstead; the Twelfth Georgia Battalion, Lieutenant Colonel Capers; and the Eighteenth Georgia Battalion, Major Basinger, was sent to Charleston, South Carolina, in consequence of movements of the enemy against Morris Island. They did not arrive in time to participate in the misfortunes of the 10th of July, when the Federals defeated our troops on the east end of the island, and gained a footing there in force. It arrived at Battery Wagner, however, about midnight of that day, except the Thirty-second Georgia Regiment, which had been left on James Island.

The troops composing the detachment had hardly been posted and lain down to seek some repose, when they were aroused to meet the attack made on the morning of the 11th. Battery Wagner was constructed with a bastioned front toward the east. The bastion on the right was covered by a piece of marsh, very boggy and overflowed by every tide. An attack from the front must, therefore, have first fallen upon the bastion on the left, which became by these circumstances, the most advanced post of the fort. It was the fortune of the Eighteenth Battalion to be posted in this bastion. The firing of our pickets as they were driven in by the enemy, brought the whole garrison to the ramparts. In the earliest dim light of the morning, the dark masses of the enemy could be descried advancing swiftly to the assault. As soon as they came within easy range, a rapid and destructive fire was opened upon them. After several desperate efforts to establish themselves, they were repulsed, and literally ran out of our fire. In this their first encounter with the enemy, the Eighteenth conducted itself with great steadiness and courage, and its loss in killed and wounded was greater than that of all the rest of the garrison. The loss of the enemy amounted to three hundred and thirty-two in killed, besides the wounded and prisoners who fell into our hands.

From the 11th until the 18th the command remained at Battery Wagner, taking its full share of all duty and labor, and enduring all the hardships, privations and sufferings peculiar to the place, with unfailing cheerfulness, it must be remembered that they were shut up in a fort of sand, without other shelter from the beams of an almost tropical sun, than an ill ventilated bomb-proof, into which from eight hundred to one thousand men were packed all day, and being in receipt of a perfect storm of shells from the enemy's ships and batteries, and of balls from his sharpshooters. There being no means of cooking provisions the men had to eat them raw, having at the same time but scanty supply of brackish water collected from holes scooped in the sand, and with no opportunity of obtaining rest, except at the imminent peril of life or limb.

The course pursued for the relief of the garrison, was to remove it at stated intervals, the worn out troops being withdrawn to James Island, Mount Pleasant or the city for rest and refreshment. But it was rest only in name, for they were called on for heavy details to work on new fortifications and to move heavy guns, and were compelled, when tired nature required its greater restorer sleep, to lie on our arms and in rank nearly every night, in readiness to repel expected attacks. Under this plan of arrangements the Eighteenth Battalion took three tours of duty at Battery Wagner during the siege, each similar in most particulars of toil and danger to the one described above. Several valuable and faithful lives were lost during our stay at Battery Wagner. On the 10th of September, 1863, the battalion was ordered to Battery Marion on Sullivan's Island, immediately adjacent to Fort Moultrie. Here it remained until late in May, 1864 bearing its full share in the incessant cannonade with which Charleston harbor resounded. The battalion was at this point engaged exclusively on artillery duty.

On the 18th of May, 1864, Major Basinger having received orders to proceed with his command to Richmond, the battalion left Battery Marion and took the route for Virginia, where it was assigned to duty at Mattox, on the Richmond and Danville railroad, to repel raiding parties of the enemy's cavalry, where it remains and is stationed at the present writing.

BATTALION AND COMPANY OFFICER.

FIELD AND STAFF.

Major W. S. Basinger, *Commanding.*
First Lieutenant E. P. Starr, *Adjutant.*
Captain R. H. Footman, *Assistant Quartermaster.*
G. W. Coxwell, *Assistant Surgeon.*

COMPANY A.

Captain T. F. Screven.
First Lieutenant W. H. Ring.
Second Lieutenant F. Tupper.
Second Lieutenant P. N. Raynal.

COMPANY B.

Captain G. W. Stiles.
First Lieutenant G. D. Smith.
Second Lieutenant W. E. Gue.
Second Lieutenant W. D. Grant.

COMPANY C.

Captain G. C. Rice.
First Lieutenant G. M. Turner.
Second Lieutenant J. R. Dillon.
Second Lieutenant E. Blois.

PRESENT STRENGTH OF BATTALION.

	Officers.	*Enlisted.*
Field and staff, ...	4	4
Company A, ...	4	97
Company B, ...	4	89
Company C, ...	4	90
Total, ...	16	280

ERRATA.–On page 120, fifth line from top, for *this* read "*his*." Same page, tenth line from top for Captain William *Arnold*, read Captain William "*Norwood*."

ADDENDUM

———

In closing up the First Volume of "Heroes and Martyrs of Georgia," &c., I desire to make a few explanations regarding the contents of the forthcoming volumes. I had hoped to be enabled to publish the Statistical and Historical Record of each Regiment from Georgia in *four* volumes; but learning from experience that the space allotted to each regiment is altogether too meagre, I have resolved to double the space allowed, that is, to fill up to *twenty* pages the record of each command, and add either to the size of the volumes or increase their number to six.

The greater portion of my MSS. having been either carried off, or destroyed by the Federals in their march through Georgia, I will be compelled to revisit the army, and re-collect the material to complete my work.

To those gentlemen who have retained copies of the record of their commands, I would respectfully request that they would forward them to me by mail; and to those who have failed to furnish me with any reports, I would say, that I should feel grateful to them if they would make them out and forward them to me.

I have remarked in my preface, that it was to me a bitter disappointment in failing to obtain more names of those who deserve a nation's praise to place on record, and I would again request that I may be furnished with the name of every man, living or dead, who has by any particular act of heroism gained a fame in his command.

I will here state, that the elegant tribute to the memory of my brother, found in the history of the Fourteenth Regiment, is from the pen of his brother in arms, Captain T. C. Moore, now Adjutant of that regiment.

I would suggest to those gentlemen who have so kindly assisted me in collecting the matter from which this work is written, that they keep a record of all casualties, &c., occurring in their respective commands, also an account of all incidents of heroism, and in fact, to keep a general commonplace book for the benefit of the future historian of their commands.

The plan of my second volume will be nearly the same as that of the first. The statistical matter will occupy the head of each history, and I would desire that its style should resemble that of the Third Georgia Regiment.

Having lost the record of every regiment which has been forwarded to me from Hood's army, I cannot promise that the history of any regiment in that army will appear in the second volume, but I will try and devote the third volume exclusively to them.

THE AUTHOR.

-- *A* --

-- *D* --

Decatur County, Ga. 10, 97
Deep Bottom, Va. 11
Dement, John J. 127, 133
Dennis, Charles J. 59
Dillon, John R. 157, 161
Donelson, Daniel Smith 143
Doolittle, Selim R. 109
Dorsey, Jasper Newton 59
Dortic, Henry S. 82
Douglas, Peyton Wade 144
Downman, William Y. (house of) 74, 87, 88
Dranesville, Va. 52, 109
Drayton, Thomas Fenwick 104, 105
Drewry's Bluff, Va. 28, 29, 37, 38, 44, 56
Duffey, Sanders J. 144
Duggan, James Barnes 123, 125, 132
Duke, John 137
Dumfries, Va. 13, 14
Duncan, Richard H. 124
Dunlap, Joseph 34
Dunn, Andrew 10
Dupree, Lewis J. 21
Durham, John A. 123, 132

-- E --

Eagle Farm, Va. 32
Early, Jubal Anderson 117, 131, 151
Eatonton, Ga. 69
Eaves, Jesse M. 153
Echols County, Ga. 124
Edray, W. Va. 143
Effingham County, Ga. 82
Eighteenth Georgia Volunteer Infantry Battalion 2, 155-161
Eighteenth Georgia Volunteer Infantry Regiment 11-19, 47, 77
Eighth Georgia Volunteer Infantry Regiment 77
Eighth North Carolina Volunteer Infantry Regiment 70
Eighth Pennsylvania Volunteer Cavalry Regiment 106
Eighty-Seventh Pennsylvania Volunteer Infantry Regiment 92
Eleventh Corps, Army of the Potomac 26
Eleventh Georgia Artillery Battalion (Cutts') 2, 108-112
Eleventh South Carolina Volunteer Infantry Regiment 64

-- *H* --

-- *K* --

Kay, William   15
Kearny, Phillip   128
Keitt, Laurence Massilon   54
Kelley, Allen   82, 85
Kellogg, Henry C.   143, 145
Kelly, James Rufus   153
Kelly, Charles C.   144, 153
Kendrick, William M.   88, 89
Kent, Thomas W.   82, 89, 144
King, Benjamin F.   41
King, William H.   157, 158
King's Landing, Va.   48
King's School House, Va.   68
Kinman, L. Marshall   124
Kinston, N. Car.   27, 36, 43, 54, 63
Knoxville, Tenn.   11, 17, 143

-- *L* --

Lake City, Fla.   28, 55, 98
Lamar, Lavoiscia L.   124
Lane, Andrew Jackson   113, 115, 124-126, 130
Lane, James Obediah   144
Lane, John   110-112
Lane, Joseph   110
Lane, Leonidas A.   145
Latimer, Thoomas   125
Laurel Hill, W. Va.   6, 7
Laurens County, Ga.   124, 143
Lawrence, James H.   104
Lawrence, James Jackson   124
Lawton, Alexander Robert   156
Lee, Augustus H.   69
Lee, Fitzhugh   117
Lee, Robert Edward   17, 19, 26, 27, 62, 74, 94, 95, 102, 105, 111, 117, 119, 120, 128, 132, 143, 147, 152
Leesburg, Va.   24, 34, 52, 62, 86, 115, 148
Lenoir Station, Tenn.   17
Lester, Richard Paul   143, 149, 151, 153
Lewis, Edward L.   120

-- *N* --

-- O --

-- P --

Patton, A. H. 13
Patton, William 55
Paulding County, Ga. 38
Paxton, William H. 144
Peiser, Sigmund 2
Pender, William Dorsey 114, 115, 117, 126, 128, 137-139
Pensacola, Fla. 6
Perdue, Hiram 146
Perry, Ga. 10
Perry, Louis C. 145, 153
Petersburg, Va. 1, 28, 29, 31, 36-38, 44-46, 56, 64-66, 68, 72, 76, 87, 91, 92, 95, 100, 111, 112, 120, 132, 139, 140
Petersburg, W. Va. 118, 151
Pettigrew, James Johnston 125, 126, 136
Philadelphia, Tenn. 17
Phillips, Alexander 69
Phillips, William 104
Phillips' Legion Cavalry Battalion 2, 104-107
Pickens County, Ga. 41
Pickett, George Edward 139
Pinckard, James S. 9
Plane, William Fisher 21, 25
Player, Samuel Thomas 118, 123, 128-131
Po River, Va. 90
Pocahontas County, W. Va. 143
Pohick Church, Va. 32
Point of Rocks, Md. 52
Point of Rocks, Va. 85
Polhill, Thomas N. 89
Polk County, Ga. 104
Pool, Benjamin G. P. 41
Pope, John 24, 73, 85, 114, 115, 128
Port Royal, Va. 26, 53, 63
Portsmouth, Va. 69, 71, 72
Potomac River 13, 15, 17, 26, 34, 43, 52, 53, 62, 86, 89, 105, 115, 129, 139, 149
Preston, William Joseph McDowell 145
Price, Felix L. 113, 115, 143-145, 149
Price, James L. 109
Pritchett, Thomas J. 100-102
Puckett, William B. C. 105, 106
Pulaski County, Ga. 124

Putnam, William D. 144, 149
Putnam County, Ga. 69, 77

-- Q --

Quincy, Fla. 97
Quitman, Ga. 98, 100
Quitman Guards 9

-- R --

Rains, Gabriel James 22, 41
Ramsay, Whiteford Smith 143, 144
Ramsey, James N. 1, 6, 8, 9
Randall, Horace D. 109
Ransom, Robert 29
Rapidan River, Va. 48, 52, 90, 111, 117, 118, 127, 131, 139
Rapidan Station, Va. 48, 90
Rappahannock River, Va. 26, 27, 34, 36, 48, 53, 54, 63, 68, 73, 105, 116, 129, 130, 135, 137, 138, 147
Rappahannock Station, Va. 48
Rawlins, Robert M. 135
Raynal, Peter N. 158, 160
Rector's Crossroads, Va. 106
Reed, Jesse 25
Reeves, James M. 45
Reid, James M. 22
Reid, James Sidney 25, 69, 72
Reno, Jesse 71
Rhodes, Edwin D. 123
Rice, Gilbert C. 157, 161
Rice, James (or Joel A.) 77
Rice, Ulysses Ashford 82, 88
Rich, William W. 105, 106
Rich Mountain, W. Va. 7
Richardson, Aaron K. 135
Richardson, Charles 110
Richmond, Va. 6, 13-15, 21-24, 27, 32-34, 36, 41, 43, 47-51, 54, 56, 59-63, 65, 66, 68, 73, 83, 84, 91, 94, 100, 108, 109, 111, 113, 118, 120, 125, 134-137, 145-147, 160
Richmond County, Ga. 9, 10, 47, 69, 82
Richmond and Danville R.R. 160

-- Y --

-- Z --